In Our Own Words

Stories of those living with,
learning from and
overcoming
the challenges of
psychogenic non-epileptic
seizures
(PNES)

Mary Martiros, M.Ed, and Lorna Myers, Ph.D.

Copyright 2015 Mary Martiros, Lorna Myers
All rights reserved.

www.createspace.com / 5659691

ISBN-13: 978-1516836482
ISBN-10: 1516836480

This book is dedicated
to all of those
who entrusted us with the
telling of their
stories,
for their honesty, their hope
and their courage.
We are
grateful and forever
changed
by your gifts
to us.

                            Mary Martiros and Lorna Myers

"The wound is the place where the Light enters you."
Rumi

Foreword

<u>In Our Own Words</u> is a project that came about when my co-author, Mary Martiros, contacted me and explained that although she had read and liked my book (Psychogenic non-epileptic seizures: A Guide), she felt that what was missing from the psychogenic non-epileptic seizures (PNES) or non-epileptic attack disorder (NEAD- as it is called in the UK) literature was a publication that allowed those living with PNES to describe this experience in their own words. As we emailed back and forth, I realized she was right. All articles and books that I was aware of were written BY professionals ABOUT persons with PNES. There was one exception (Lowering the Shield), a book written by a spouse of someone who lives with PNES, but again, this was not the person living with PNES speaking.

So, the project was born and we began by creating a questionnaire that would allow respondents to tell us about the road they traveled to their diagnosis of PNES and after. We were interested in hearing why respondents thought they had these seizures, experiences good and bad with health professionals, family and friends along the way, what had been the most helpful to them or what they thought they might need, what, if anything, they had learned from PNES, what they would like to communicate to others and how they saw their future. The questionnaire was bounced back and forth to make sure we had fine-tuned it as much as possible. It was decided that we would put a call out through the various PNES Facebook pages and through a PNES blog post. The book project was also announced at the first annual PNES conference held in New Jersey in September of 2014.

Volunteers contacted me from all over the US (New York, New Jersey, Missouri, Texas, Kansas, Minnesota, Maine, Connecticut, and Hawaii) which was excellent news because this seemed to add an enriching aspect to the book in that we might see if experiences with PNES differ across the nation. And then, volunteers from across the world also stepped up, including a country in the Caribbean, Australia, the United Kingdom, the Netherlands, South Africa, and even one young lady from Japan.

An appointment was set up with each volunteer for a phone interview. The questionnaire was sent beforehand so that the respondents were familiar with the questions and prepared. They were permitted to withdraw from the project at any time, no explanations needed. One volunteer formally withdrew after completing the interview and two others did not respond to an email request to approve the final interview write-up and were as such considered to have withdrawn. In total, 19 complete interviews were collected for this book. Mary and I decided that no medical institutions or health professionals would be named in order to protect the privacy of the participants and all who were involved with their treatment.

The two of us felt it was very important that the approach to the interview should be open-ended and that the interviewer should be as unobtrusive as possible. By this we mean, we wanted these interviews to be the words of the volunteers and not the interviewers'. As a clinical psychologist, this was an interesting and sometimes difficult experience for me since I am often inclined to jump in with follow-up questions or interpretations, but I managed to reign myself in and eventually even came to enjoy this form of interviewing.

As I mentioned, I am a clinical psychologist and I have been working with PNES for over ten years. I expected to know much of what volunteers would share with me since I speak with patients

every day. I felt I was well aware of many of the challenges patients face with our health care system and society as a whole. So, as you might imagine, I was quite surprised with how profoundly moved I was when I conducted the interviews and then read each finalized testimonial. I was struck by how poignant each testimonial was, how similar some aspects were and how unique others were. As might be expected, most volunteers had experienced trauma of one form or another, but there were also a handful that represented those who develop PNES without having traumatic experiences. It was intriguing to see the differences and yet, similarities between every testimonial.
And undeniably, I was impressed with the bravery and resilience

that each volunteer exhibited since it was clear that reflecting on these questions and reading and approving the final version of a testimonial was hard. But one after another, the volunteers expressed that they felt it was essential to do this in hopes of making a difference in the lives of those who live with PNES and to improve the present woeful way in which persons with PNES are misunderstood and treated.

I now invite you to continue reading this book and to reflect on the life changing experience of PNES as explained by those who live with, struggle with, and survive PNES.

Lorna Myers, Ph.D.

August 2015

Acknowledgements

I would like to thank Urmi Vaidya-Mathur, LCSW of the Northeast Regional Epilepsy Group for her tremendous help in conducting interviews and for having helped with her valuable insights about the initial questionnaire. I would also like to thank Go Taniguchi, M.D., Ph.D., Assistant Professor of the Department of Neuropsychiatry in the University of Tokyo Hospital, for providing an invaluable interview of a young Japanese woman living with PNES. Finally, I would like to express my thanks to research assistant at the Northeast Regional Epilepsy Group, Jace Jones, BS, for his crucial help in transcribing interviews.

Introduction

I have experienced a lifetime of illness as a result of traumatic sexual, physical and emotional abuse. It is important to understand at the outset, that victims of abuse and other traumatic experiences, need to be able to express their feelings about their resulting trauma without feeling implicated as somehow complicit in the acts forced upon them.

This, however, often becomes the case and survivors of extreme abuse and trauma are silenced before they ever have the chance to share their pain, anger or innocence. They become victims, not only of their abusers or of the events which caused their trauma, but of the judgments of a society too afraid to look at such heinous crimes against children for what they really are.

Until we, as protectors of our children and as a world with a conscience toward eradicating these unthinkable actions realize this, children will continue to be molested, beaten and raped.

Today, I, and many others like me, still relive the traumas experienced during childhood, through dissociative (non-epileptic) seizures and PTSD, both of which cripple our lives into isolation, inactivity, depression and, often, total despair.

Resulting psychological disorders like PNES are the mind's way of protecting survivors from traumatic memories resulting from real and horrific childhood events. No one 'fakes' these seizures, as has often been stated by so many professionals and nonprofessionals alike.

On the following pages are the stories of some of the most courageous people you will ever meet. They are not victims, but heroes of their own lives. They may have been violated physically or traumatized emotionally but their spirits are intact and their courage is apparent. Despite whatever trauma they have endured, they are living lives of purpose and of strength.

I hope that you can read this book with your compassionate heart. We have all been gifted with a compassionate heart.

Many Blessings,
Mary Martiros

*You are important
and you matter.
Your feelings matter,
your voice matters,
your story matters,
your life matters.
Always.*

AP
New York
November 2014

AP is a 36 year old, married woman with two school aged children. She is currently unemployed and on disability but prior to her diagnosis of PNES she earned her bachelor's degree in education She left her current job after a car accident in 2008.

Diagnostic history:
My seizures began when I was 24. I found myself awake in a hospital room after my husband heard a noise coming from the room. He came in and noticed that I had fallen to the floor and then called EMS. They took me to the local hospital where I was kept for a few days. At first they thought that I might have epilepsy but didn't start me on any medication. So I went back home and to work but I started to realize that there were situations where I was "losing time" and had "no conscious realization" of what was going on or what I was doing. From 2002 to 2005 I saw 4 different neurologists. Each started me on different medications (Dilantin, Topamax, Keppra, Lamictal) and made different diagnoses. After three long years of working with all these different doctors I ended up being admitted from the ER and hooked up to a VEEG. That's where I met with the epilepsy specialist who told me that he believed I had PNES after five days in the hospital. He then sent me for neuropsychological testing and I ended up having the diagnosis of PNES confirmed. Each time I met with a different specialist in this center, I was educated about what PNES was and finally I was also referred for PNES therapy.

This was so different from other experiences I had before. In the past, I was told I was "faking it". I was also told that my migraines were causing the episodes. Many of my doctors barely spoke with me. They tried different medications with no follow up when I told them that I was still having seizures. Can you believe I was never hooked up for a VEEG until I met with the specialist even though I had seen a bunch of neurologists? It used to be just a 20 minute EEG in an office and based on that, they decided how to treat me. A lot of doctors, then and now, are fully unaware of PNES and very dismissive when I explain PNES to them. But I have to say, that it seems like some of the newer doctors seem to be a bit more interested in learning about PNES.

Do you know why you have PNES?
I sincerely don't know why. I have a high quality of life and a strong support system. Prior to my first seizure, things in my life were going well. I was recently married and had just graduated from college. I had no trauma and wasn't anxious about anything. In many ways I had a "very blessed life".

Is there anything that exacerbates your seizures?

I do feel that stress is a major factor. Currently my biggest source of stress is financial followed by raising two little children. I have also noticed that when I have a series of migraines or if I get sick with a cold or anything, I am more likely to experience an episode.

Is there anything you would like to tell your family and friends about PNES?

Not really. I am blessed to have a very active and positive support system that is well educated on PNES. My friends are also very helpful and supportive. I do feel that it would be "easier" to have a more visible illness to explain to others, or one that is more understood. It is hard, at times, to describe and explain PNES with strangers. It's also hard because there is no warning for my next episode. Some other illnesses have "clues" to tell you that you may suffer from a flare up of the condition. It is the unknown that I really find very difficult to deal with.

What would you like to tell others about PNES?
It sucks sometimes to deal with this, there are days when you are depressed and you can't do anything but you have to lean on your support system and you have to sort of get over it. Sometimes you are not going to be able to perform at 100% and you can't always control the feelings and interactions you have with others because they do not know or understand PNES but at the end of the day you have to live your life. The best thing you can do for yourself is try to get to a group of professionals who know how to treat PNES and who will treat you with respect.

Elliott (this is not his real name)
New Jersey
November 2014

Elliott is a 53 year old man who is married and has 2 step children and 7 step grandchildren (the oldest is 23 years old and the youngest is 10 years old). He holds a certification that is akin to an Associate's degree in business. He is currently receiving Disability Benefits.
This interview was conducted with Elliott and his wife.

Diagnostic History

I think I may have had my first psychogenic seizure (PNES) in my early teens. But I had my first epileptic seizure at 18 months. My father told me that he walked in and saw I was having a seizure and my mother was just standing over my crib looking and not doing anything for me. As a kid, I had seizures all over-at home, out of the home, everywhere. Basically, if this happened in school, they would call whoever was caring for me at the time to come to the school to pick me up. I don't remember being bullied or teased over my seizures. I had all sorts of tests as a child - I remember having EEG probes (needles) at the time were stuck under the scalp. Then I had an occipital lobectomy when I was 28 and I had a vagal nerve stimulator (VNS) when I was 42.

In May 2005, I traveled out of state and entered a new medication trial and after I had a Video-EEG, the doctor was belligerent when he spoke to me. He basically said that I was faking for attention and that I did not even need my service dog. He told me that I was not an epileptic and "never will be." We talked about my trauma history and he said I needed to seek out therapy. Shortly, they took me off all my medications, my neurologist totally agreed with him, and in December of that same year I had status epilepticus. My seizure lasted half an hour, my wife called 911, they took me to the emergency room (ER) and I spent 11 days in the hospital. Ever since that time, I knew I felt something was different. Just could not put my finger on it. My neurologist was very concerned and sympathetic after that.

What are your psychogenic seizures like?

They start with minor, left-sided tremors, weakness in my legs, then, violent shaking and rapid back and forth motion of my head. I'm able to speak and communicate but can't remember after. One of my cats senses it and sticks with me before, during and after. When I recover I am a little disoriented for a few minutes. The shortest ones are ten minutes and the longest was 14 hours. Wife: I can tell when he is going to have a PNES about half an hour before. He has a "look" on his face, his behavior and talk changes.

Since having PNES, I have neuropathy on the left side. I have to use thick, arthritis cutlery so I can eat on my own. His wife explains: Otherwise, it is humiliating to be out for a meal and to have to ask me to cut the food for him. People sometimes don't realize how important independence is.

Do you know why you have these seizures?

My mother was the main contributor. When my mother and father divorced, she remarried, and then divorced again. She had a female roommate that was very abusive to me, not to my younger siblings, just to me. My mother watched what was happening to me and ignored it and did not intervene. I don't understand how a parent can do that. My father tried to get in contact with me over the years and she never gave me the information. I don't have a single positive memory of my mother. Can you believe I don't have a single "comfort food?" My mother was a psychiatric nurse. She should have known better. Some think that this may have been Münchausen by proxy. I was in foster care from the age of 12 to 14. I was shuffled around to many homes. Foster care was for the most part ok. Then when I was 13 my mother basically said you'll never see me again if I didn't go back with her, so I left foster care. I went back home and took the abuse some more. When I was 16 years old, I went back to foster care and I was raped.

Experience with medical professionals

I have felt total negativity. There are times when doctors have just walked out of the room. Nurses, interns, doctors are just not interested. I have had said to me in the ER: "When you're done, you can go home." I can't even mention my PNES to my neurologist. She's not interested. She doesn't want to discuss it and says "talk to your therapist." My therapist understands and validates me. Most of the doctors still call them "pseudoseizures," you say "PNES" and a lot of them don't know what that is.

What contributes to your episodes?

The stress going on at the time. My quality of life is very bad. Out of a 0-100, I would say it's -30 (laugh). I can't do things I used to do when I was just an epileptic, like volunteering and riding my bike. I had volunteered and participated in fundraisers for about 30 years. When I apply for volunteer jobs I don't get a call back. We lost all our friends and my family since I got the diagnosis of PNES.

I have accepted the diagnosis but I have difficulty with the pain. It is much more intense than with the epileptic seizures. It has taken a big toll on my body. I was also diagnosed with fibromyalgia after I was diagnosed with PNES. I used to go to the Wellness Center but the staff needed to keep an eye on me and I am too much of a liability. We live on a third floor walk-up so that's my exercise now. I also really try not to think about my mother because as soon as she puts her foot in the door in my brain...

What helps you cope with your PNES?

The thing that helps me cope the most: My wife! I also get support from my grandkids. My wife and I take cabs or walk. That's why we live here because things are within walking distance. Sometimes we go to Philly, to a local aquarium, we take the bus and we enjoy that.

At first I clashed with my therapist because I was in denial. I do talk therapy with her one time per week. It seems like lately she is picking my brain for information (laugh) but definitely she has helped me with "think before you speak." She hasn't helped me with my seizures or with my depression and anxiety though. It would be really nice to be able to talk to others who have this too. I have asked my neurologist and she says that she doesn't have any other patients with PNES. Although her receptionist says that she does. When I went to the PNES conference in September it was so good to see all the others with PNES. I got to meet someone I have been "friends" with on a PNES Facebook page for 10 years.

Family/friends reactions:

All our mutual friends have disappeared-the phone calls went down, the visits went down and then completely stopped. Now we have no friends and no social activities. It's like when I was diagnosed with PNES, they felt I was "faking it." My brother and sister act like we are "dirt on the welcome mat" because we don't work and they look down on us.

Others are judgmental or just don't care. I had a seizure in a parking lot and was laying on the ground and people just drove around me and no one stopped. I used to help people, now whenever I ask for help; they slam the door in my face. So why should I bother helping?

What would you like to tell others in your life, your family, your friends and your medical professionals, about what it's like to live with PNES and what they can do to help you to heal from this illness?

I would like for my family to accept me for who I am. I am so distant from my family. My mom is deceased. I'm not sure if my dad really understands PNES, or if he really wants to, either. I feel so empty sometimes. What biological family I do have, very rarely, if ever return phone calls. (crying). His wife steps in and says: I would want to say: take a moment and listen. This isn't a thing to get attention. It's tearing him apart and damaging his body. Be there to listen.

It would be nice to work in PNES awareness. Wife: I don't think awareness will happen in our lifetimes. It would be nice to say "PNES" and for a person to say: "Oh, yes, I have heard of it." Or for a doctor to say: "Let me help you."

CN
Midwest
12/08/2014

Profile: CN is a 56 year-old female with two adult stepchildren from her husband's previous marriage and 2 adult foster children. She has two Master's degrees and is currently employed, part time, as a minister.

History

I began having unusual brain activity around the time that I was getting married. I felt like I was breaking family rules and expectations that I would always remain a single woman – the sweet youngest daughter 'destined' to become the helper to others in the family – but without a family of my own.

I became engaged to be married in early January, 1992 and had my first seizure-like experience in late January of the same year. For the 3 days before my first seizure, I felt very sleepy and like I couldn't breathe well. I yawned deeply and repeatedly, and felt like I was in a daze.

Then, while at a restaurant with colleagues on an out-of-town business trip, I passed out. Those present at the time reported that I fainted onto the dinner table, and was unresponsive for about 10 minutes with my eyes open. When I regained consciousness, the EMT's were there checking my vital signs, etc. They released me and a colleague drove me back to my hotel where I remained panicky for the remainder of the night. Later that night I learned that another colleague at the same dinner had died suddenly of an apparent heart attack. Did we both have some strange food poisoning? Did I faint due to some subconscious premonition that a colleague would die that night? Was I having a panic attack? A nervous breakdown? Or did I simply faint, like most good southern ladies do now and then?

When I returned home from this business trip, I saw my primary care physician who ordered a CAT scan. The results were inconclusive – so she directed me not to drive and referred me to a local neurologist. The neurologist ordered additional tests – and then met with me and asked me if I had ever had a "nervous breakdown." His use of that phrase frightened me terribly – and I elected to go to another neurologist at a nearby, well-known medical center. This second neurologist had a world-class reputation and I felt a high level of trust in him.

This neurologist ordered a sleep study, and said that the results had indicated some epileptic-form spikes. Based on the results of that sleep study, he prescribed Tegretol. I did not like the various side effects of Tegretol: my vision was blurry, I felt I was in a deep fog, and generally did not feel like myself.

I was allowed to resume driving – but recall that on at least one occasion had a strong panic reaction while driving – being flooded with thoughts and images of my impending death. I stopped the car, and called for someone to come drive me home.

Several other times during the next 6-12 months, I got pronounced tingling down the left side of my body, deep hot flashes (I was 10+ years pre-menopause at the time), and felt like I would faint at any moment. I also experienced my thoughts as being "very jumpy." I had a prevailing sense that I was 'trying' to act like my normal self, but inside was jumpy and fragmented.

I was never given a definitive diagnosis.

After some months of unsuccessful treatment with Tegretol, my neurologist prescribed imipramine – an old school anti-depressant. The imipramine seemed helpful – and I began to feel 'like myself' again. I remained on imipramine for approximately 1 ½ years.

Quality of life

My life felt unmanageable for approximately 2 years, from 1992-1994.

A combination of the anti-depressant, and setting boundaries with my husband's ex-wife who had been intrusive in our lives, were both very helpful.

I have been asymptomatic since 1994 – but have received effective treatment for clinical depression since that that time.

Support
My husband and family were very supportive in helping me through this difficult time.

Parting words:
How you look on the outside doesn't always match the feelings inside. I now take care of myself and set boundaries with others that work for me.

Maya
Massachusetts
12/05/2015

Maya is a 59 year old woman. She has been married for 35 years and has three children and three grandchildren. She has been unemployed for eight years and has been on disability for three years.

At what age or in what year did your seizures begin?

Non epileptic seizures began at age 43. Epileptic seizures began at age 19.

Do you know why you have these seizures?

The seizures are caused by triggers from my past trauma of abuse and also by current stressful situations in my life.

How was your diagnosis made and how was it explained to you by that doctor?

I had a 3 day video EEG at age 54 and was told that I had "pseudoseizures" and that there was nothing that could be done for me. Then the epileptologist told me that I "could tell them to go away".

How long was it from the time your seizures began until they were diagnosed?

It was 11 years before my disorder was diagnosed. During that time I was put on many medications which only served to render me incoherent most of the time. The doctors I saw were essentially guessing at what was wrong with me.

What do your seizures look like? How do they present themselves?

Sometimes I stare off or close my eyes and am paralyzed but fully conscious.
Sometimes my speech becomes distorted, my thoughts become very confused and my motor functioning is compromised.
Sometimes I have seizures when I'm sleeping and these are very violent. I yell and cry and thrash around and they come out of nowhere. Other times I have seizures from noise or from music. I had epileptic seizures from noise also so I don't know if these are epileptic or PNES.

How do you feel after your seizures and what is your recovery time (minutes, hours, days)?

I usually feel upset and tired. It takes an hour or 2 for me to recover from a mild seizure and up to 2 days to recover from days when they come repeatedly.

Were you diagnosed with another disorder or illness prior to being diagnosed with PNES?

I had a nonmalignant brain tumor which started undiagnosed temporal lobe seizures at age 19. 13 years later I had a grand mal seizure and they found the tumor. I was never diagnosed with epilepsy until after they found the tumor, though I had been to several neurologists and other specialists.

**What has been your experience in working with medical professionals, (doctors, nurses, ER physicians, EMT's, psychiatrists, neurologists, psychologists, social workers, etc.).
Give examples if you have some.**

I have been largely negated in my experiences. When I was having epileptic seizures from a tumor that couldn't be seen on a CAT scan, I was told that my 'episodes' were the cause of me being emotionally disturbed by two different neurologists. I was refused treatment for PNES at two different emergency rooms in the past 3 years. One doctor said that she couldn't treat me even though I had had 7 seizures that day because I was 'non emergent'. The other doctor said that he was refusing me treatment because I was 'faking' my seizures. He, then, spit in my face in the ER. I reported him to patient advocacy at the hospital but they refused to address the incident. In both instances I had been sent to the emergency room by my doctor.

Have you felt heard, understood or validated by the medical profession as a whole?

No. I have been dismissed as someone with a condition that I will "probably always have" and I don't believe that that is true. I think doctors say this because they don't have a definitive answer and it is an extremely hurtful thing to say to people with PNES. No one has the right to cast down a life sentence on a disorder where the outcome carries so many variables with it. I haven't gotten this response from my counselors or my family doctor but from my neurologist and from my counseling psychologist. These professionals should know better. Trying to Play God does not serve their patients well.

How would you rate or describe your quality of life?

My life is very blessed. I have a wonderful husband and amazing children and 3 beautiful grandchildren. I have a beautiful home and plenty of everything I need. Most importantly, I have a very strong connection to Spirit. I'm a Reiki Master/Teacher and I do healing work when called upon to help others. I get frustrated, at times, because I feel very isolated when I have seizures. I used to be a teacher and a developmental specialist in early intervention, I am a musician but I can no longer perform, I am a writer so I try to keep writing but sometimes I get bogged down with illness. I try, always, to bring myself back to the present moment and to accept where I am in that moment and when I do that everything else falls into place. That is how I find my peace.

What benefits you the most when coping with your seizures (in avoiding them and dealing with them when they are happening)?

I know that stress plays a big part in my seizures so I am trying to eliminate it from my life as much as possible. I've realized that I don't breathe deeply unless I make a conscious effort to do so and when I do it helps me greatly. Putting myself first has always been difficult for me but I am doing that now and it is tremendously helpful in reducing my seizures. The word NO has become the biggest word in the English language for me. It's a great word and I'm learning to use it often. In conversations that are upsetting, I've learned to say, "I can't talk about this anymore right now. I need to take a break", and I leave the room. I've learned that I am not responsible for the welfare of everyone I love. I have learned to put myself first. I'm also getting okay with people not liking me. I usually don't like them very much either.

What exacerbates your seizures?

When I feel threatened I have seizures. I have PTSD and when memories from my past are triggered I often have seizures. I've been in counseling for 34 years so I'm much better at coping with it now but trauma runs pretty deep so I have to work at it constantly. Doctors who are dismissive trigger my seizures, family members and friends who are aloof and uncaring or judgmental also trigger me.

Do you feel that you have the understanding and support of your friends and family in dealing with your illness?

Some people in my family are very supportive and understanding. My husband, one of my daughters and one of my sisters are very understanding and supportive. My other 2 children don't want to talk about my illness with me and no one else really gets it in my family. I don't have any friends who I can speak to about my illness.

What would you like to tell others in your life, your family, your friends and your medical professionals, about what it's like to live with PNES and what they can do to help you to heal from this illness?

I have wished, for many years, that everyone I know and every doctor I have ever dealt with could live my life for just one day. I know that this isn't possible but, if it were, then I know that I would never have to try to explain anything to any of them about what it's like to have PNES. I wouldn't have to try to convey how frightening and disorienting and uncertain my life is. I wouldn't have to tell them how depressed I get when I can't leave my house for weeks at a time. I wouldn't have to explain my exhaustion or the feeling that my life lacks any purpose at all or that when I have seizures all day long for months at a time, I go to bed at night and pray that I won't wake up in the morning. They would understand. And that would help me heal. Their understanding and compassion would help me heal.

What have you learned, personally, from having PNES?

I feel that the biggest thing I have learned from having PNES is to have an open heart.

We all experience pain of one kind or another. Pain, to me, has been a teacher. It has allowed me to be aware of the pain in other people and to grow in compassion for others. I cannot ignore other people or animals in pain, whether it be physical, mental or emotional because I have experienced extraordinary amounts of pain in my illness. I don't know how much pain others experience but I do know that when someone is in pain they need our compassion in that moment because, in that moment, their pain is all-consuming. The other valuable lesson I have learned from PNES is acceptance. Accepting my circumstance and my life as it is, in every moment, has brought me peace and freedom.

Other comments…

Healing begins with loving yourself first. That is where all healing begins.

*Let go of worry,
Let go of fear.
Let go of the
pains and
journeys,
however reckless,
which others insist
upon.*

                          The Book of Love

JJ
January 2015
Kansas

JJ is a 22 year old young woman who is single and has no children. She is a college graduate and lives by herself. She is currently receiving Disability Benefits for an unrelated medical condition. She had been trying to go through the work program offered by Social Security but since it was taking longer than expected, she decided to look for a job on her own. She was going on a job interview that she found on Craig's List the day after this interview took place and if not successful, she was considering returning to in-home health care which is where she worked for 5 years.

Diagnostic History

My seizures began when I was 8 years old, but we didn't know what they were, we thought they were panic attacks. Then they got really bad when I was 16, then stopped, and then they got really bad again when I was 21 or 22 (a year ago). I was diagnosed by a neurologist in my hometown but I really got confirmation of the diagnosis when I traveled out of state. I came out and did the EEG. My local doctor hadn't done that yet, the neurologist thought it PNES but the psychologist thought it was epilepsy and so they were tossing me back and forth. I was having close to 40 or more seizures a day.

It wasn't until I traveled out of state that the diagnosis was confirmed through Video-EEG. Before being diagnosed with PNES, I was diagnosed with depression, PTSD, autism, an eating disorder, substance abuse, and anxiety. I also have Crohn's Disease, GERD and some food sensitivities.

What are your psychogenic seizures like?

My seizures cause me to convulse. I will often have problems with my vision and hearing; they may be gone for up to five minutes. This happens in almost all of my seizures. My seizures used to last up to 15 to 20 minutes now they last 5 minutes max, sometimes 8 minutes more recently.

When I was getting better, I stopped losing my hearing and sight. I would still convulse but I could still see and hear everything else going on, but now I'm back to not being able to hear or see sometimes during a seizure. I have two kinds of seizures: one feels like a real seizure and then others that feel like a flashback of when I was traumatized.

When the seizure is over, I feel exhausted, I normally recover fairly quickly. Lately, I haven't been recovering as quickly as I used to and sometimes my vision will be absent long after the seizure has stopped. I've been trying to teach my psychologist sign language but that hasn't been going too well (laugh). Sometimes I can write if I can see.

Do you know why you have these seizures?

It was explained to me that my seizures were caused by PTSD and trauma, and that they could be quelled and worked through with a specific type of therapy. I believe my alcoholism played a big role in it too, when I stopped drinking they got worse. The doctors who diagnosed me spoke about alcohol as a kind of self- medication. Now I am drinking again and I'm having the seizures again. Now

I think it's that I'm drinking <u>because</u> I have the seizures. My seizures are tied into the trauma, into the PTSD and the alcohol. There's no such thing as "mindful drinking" (laugh). It's going to ruin anything positive that I put into my life. I'm trying to fill a void that cannot be filled, I have to face it which I am doing with the help of AA and my team of Psychologists, and Psychiatrists. I have noticed since I have been sober that the seizures were worse in the beginning and have tapered off again. So for me there is a big connection.

What has your experience with medical professionals been like?

Not very good. I was in psychiatric treatment since I was 3 years old, receiving medication. I went through CBT, DBT, EMDR, group therapy, family therapy, hypnotherapy, all kinds of talk therapy. I was seen by social workers at least twice a week, sometimes even three times a week at my home as a kid. I was in special education (I was put in a classroom with kids who for lack of a better word really needed to be in there and I didn't). Some even had Down's syndrome. I was hospitalized many times but I never received much help.

With PNES, I struggled for a long time with being tossed back and forth between medical professionals. I was also told many times I was faking it for attention or medication not only in the emergency room and by my neurologist, also by my therapist, and psychiatrist. ER doctors specifically told me and my Mom that I was faking these for medication. It was pretty devastating to hear and for my mom to hear. I also have had people in the ER rip my clothes off of me, emergency medical staff screaming at me "If you don't stop it now I'm going to tear your clothes off. " I guess they were doing this to get me to respond or stop or something and then she cut my shirt and I was aware that she was doing that but I couldn't do anything to stop her. My first neurologist told me that there was really no help for me. He told me that I needed a caretaker at home. For months and months and months I felt like there was no hope and I didn't want that for myself. Then my mom luckily found a book on PNES and for the first time in months I had a little hope. Until then it was a struggle for someone to take me seriously. I wanted help and was not finding any at that time in-state.

Have any experiences with medical professionals been positive and what about them was helpful?

Until I was 16, none of the experiences I had were positive. In fact, they were all invalidating. And it's only when I starting seeing my psychologist at 16 years; that was my first positive experience. And um that's why I've kept her around (laugh).

At 13, I stopped all medications because I was on 14 medications and I was drugged out of my mind. I started taking medication again when I got sober but then the psychiatrist drugged me up again. I was on 9 different medications before I found the psychiatrist I have now. She's been the only positive experience I've had with psychiatry. She is a wonderful doctor and I am so grateful for her.

I feel like I did my most beneficial and helpful work last year with a psychologist who specializes in PNES using exposure therapy. My life greatly improved since then. I wouldn't have a life, I really wouldn't. That treatment gave me hope, let me know I'm not alone, and helped me realize that this isn't something that I wished for or could have predicted; that it's something that happened and that there was light at the end of the tunnel. But when I went back home, I encountered many professionals who were rude, demeaning, and who didn't grasp PNES. Luckily, I recently found someone who's kind, understanding and specializes in exposure treatment. She is a very well educated doctor and acknowledges my

capacity as a client which is very important.

What contributes to your episodes?

Stress is the number one thing as well as trauma. I've noticed my seizures have increased because I'm under so much stress now. Moving is really stressful, having a sexual offender come back twice into my life is really stressful, not having a job is really stressful, losing my sobriety has been stressful. Trying to get that sobriety back has been stressful. And losing a lot of friendships. As I have started working through more of my trauma, I notice that my seizures amp up and then they taper off as I become more exposed to the trauma in treatment.

Have you experienced any changes since developing PNES?

I have more fear of doing things than I used to like going out dancing, going to the store or being out at night or driving. At least during the day I can see what's going on.

I also have more memory problems than I used to. Sometimes people will be talking to me and I will be like "What were we talking about" and I'm like "where did I go?"

Before finding help, my quality of life was nil. Having 40 seizures a day didn't leave room for much. My quality of life is much better now. I can get out, I can work out, I can live alone, and I am looking into employment. I feel like I have a better grasp on how my seizures present themselves and a better handle on why they're there and they just aren't out of nowhere.

What helps you cope with your PNES?

Breathing. It is ingrained in me now from my treatment. Journaling, all the journaling one of my psychologists had me do made a lot of sense as to where a lot of things correlated. Also, when I went back through it recently I saw that different things that happened during the day would trigger old emotion. Other things that are helpful: Hearing someone's voice during the seizure, using ice to ground myself, trying to feel the carpet if I can't see. Feeling what's around me. If I can't hear, looking at what's around me. Then also talking to myself is helpful. I say in my head "you're safe, you're okay." Oh and petting my cat is also helpful (laugh).

How would you describe your family and friends reaction to your PNES?

I've had a really hard time not just with medical professionals, but also friends. I lost a lot of very fundamental support prior to being diagnosed and after being diagnosed.

A lot of my other friends, that I used to hang out with and thought I was close with, don't want to hang out with me anymore because I have seizures. They don't know how to handle it and they don't believe in <u>my</u> capacity to be able to handle it regardless of what I say. Or they have become scared. Even my mom still freaks out during my seizures. I often need to express to her "I've been having these for like a year and a half now and am more capable of handling them than I used to be." And she is learning now that I can handle them much better than I used to. I honestly wouldn't be where I am at without the support she has continuously given me. It's been a struggle especially because I was so used to having people to call, or lean on and the two people I do still have live really far now. One of them lives about an hour away and she's working 90 hours a week with a baby and my only other friend lives about 45 minutes away, but she's pregnant right now and she's not been feeling good.

I had a lot more support months ago than I do now, which has been hard and hurtful. Most of my support comes from my therapists, doctors and my mom. I am currently looking for meet-up groups and more opportunities to meet other people since I have been feeling better. I also had a lot of support through my online schooling and I am thinking about going back to school for that reason. It's a very healing school.

What would you like to tell others in your life, your family, your friends and your medical professionals, about what it's like to live with PNES and what they can do to help you to heal from this illness?

That PNES is not something one can just create, that it is an illness and should be treated as such. Number one thing: They are not fake. I want more mental health professionals to have more awareness of what PNES is and for it not to be called "pseudo seizures."

My advice for therapists is: don't freak out, be patient, and be kind. I really don't like the word "pseudo" because it implies fake and I've had to correct numerous doctors on that 'cause it drives me nuts (laugh)!

I would also say that you need to take it on a one day at a time basis and that it's hard not to know what each day will be like. That I'm okay, that they're not epileptic and that I've learned to keep myself safe, that I've lived on my own when I was having a lot of these a day. I've learned to take it one day at a time and to be gentler with myself. I've learned to understand that this isn't something that I created or asked for, it's just something that happened due to trauma, and it can get better.

I would like to tell my psychologist that she can still work with me, even though I'm having seizures. I feel like that's the thing a lot of therapists don't grasp. Just because the patient has a seizure doesn't mean that for the rest of the session they're absent. One of my psychologists thinks that if I have a seizure, because seizures are a form of disassociation that I'm completely gone for the rest of the session, and that's not true. I'm still able to come back and be present for the rest of the session. I would tell my other psychologist that I'm very grateful for her patience, her knowledge, that she's willing to work <u>with</u> me, and that she recognizes me as an individual and treats me as an individual, not as a group. As for that first neurologist, I would tell him "Don't ever tell a patient that there's no hope, there's always hope, there's always a chance." I'm lucky that I was able to find it but "I could have taken your word for it and doomed myself."

What do you see in your future?

Short term, I'm moving, I'm going to get a job, I'm going to continue to fight and get better. I also want to try to start a group for people in my hometown who have PNES. I think it's something that needs to happen. It's nice to have face to face contact and for others to know that there's help out there.

So long term, I want to study to become a Neuropsychologist. I want to help others who have PNES, and I have always loved Psychology. I've always wanted to do psychology, since I was 10. I used to read the psychology dictionary, and by this I mean study it all because I found it so interesting. I just never knew which field to pursue. I feel I could utilize a lot of my prior schooling, which is also important to me. Whether or not I will have the opportunity to do this mentally and physically is not clear now, but it would be my ultimate goal. I really feel that there needs to be more neuropsychologists out there because there's just not enough who specialize and understand PNES and the treatment that it entails. My future is bright, no matter what I do, I want to make a difference in this world and I will.

NB
Netherlands

February 2015

NB is a 21 year old single young woman who has been in a relationship for the past four and a half years. She is in her second year of college completing her three year Bachelor degree and is then planning to go on to obtain a Master's degree. She is currently a full-time student and has been working about 8 to 10 hours a week at her school for the past 4 months. Prior to this she worked for 6 years about 8 to 10 hours a week at a supermarket.

Diagnostic History
I had my first seizure at 17 years of age, almost 4 years ago. The day before I remember I went to the swimming pool. It was a pretty busy day and the day after I was having lunch in the break my body started shaking out of nowhere. I used to have the tendency that when I didn't eat regularly I got shaky. So I just thought "okay maybe it's just that, I need to eat a bit and it will pass." But the day after, it happened again and then I went to the doctor. It didn't stop. My whole body was shaking, I was conscious and the doctor looked at me and was like "I have no idea what this is." And then he called his colleague and they looked at me as if I were a monkey or something and they didn't have a clue. So, they gave me some beta blockers. I took them but a week later I was sitting in my History class and ˍraised my hand to call the teacher to say "sir I'm not really feeling well" and that's basically the last thing I remember. That time I became unconscious and had my first real seizure. And then we went to the first aid in the hospital and then just waited because basically they didn't really know what was wrong. So then the tests started, it took weeks, I actually had a

seizure during the EEG. They didn't see anything, and at that point the story just ends for the neurologist. It's like he could conclude "okay you're healthy physically, I cannot help you anymore, see you later." It is very frustrating because from the moment you go into this hospital they don't really get you. As soon as it appears that it's not something physical, you're basically done and they just want you out. They show you the door. So, you even get desperate sometimes. My experience with the medical field has not been that good. So, I kept having seizures and a while later, my mom was in the hospital because she had a broken leg and there was a nurse who she was talking with and she mentioned me and the problems I was having. Coincidentally, this nurse knew of a specialist at the epilepsy center. She encouraged us to get an appointment there. When I saw that specialist, he diagnosed me with "psychogenic non-epileptic seizures." Basically, he explained "it's psychologically linked" and recommended I start treatment. Treatment was really basic because I was still in high school and I was in my senior year and I really wanted to pass high school so they decided not to dig deeper into my emotions, because that wouldn't benefit me at that time. The fact that I passed my exams is a miracle of miracles. Then my mom just sat me down and said "listen honey, you're not gonna go to college this year. I'm sorry your friends are going to go, it's gonna be really tough. But you can't. You are tired, you need treatment, it's not going to happen. So I stayed behind and I kept working at the supermarket, despite having seizures there every day, but, I needed the rhythm work gave me and they were really understanding, fortunately. And at that time I started the search for a good psychologist. The epilepsy clinic didn't really help in this matter, because they simply don't know where to direct you. I remember at one point I was just desperately sitting at my internist's office crying and I really didn't want to go any further anymore. So then you end up knocking on doors basically saying "Hi I have this thing, they call 'non epileptic seizures,' can you help me?" and a lot of psychologists, said "no, because it's something that seems physical and I don't dare to treat you." But then after a while I found a really good psychologist and I started treatment. She was clear with me that she didn't know about PNES but she was willing to learn about it and I really appreciate that she did that. I think she had a really good vision of what was needed very soon even without knowing the term PNES, and that it was indeed childhood trauma in combination with my personal character that caused these seizures. Also she taught me techniques. When I used to feel sad or not well I used to turn inside and she literally made me turn outwards. We would stand up and push on something physically. Also, she taught me how to breathe differently. I used to breathe with my chest which is really bad and she taught me to practice breathing differently.

What is your understanding of why you have these seizures?

Well when they started I obviously didn't know because they are so physical in appearance that I thought either I had epilepsy or multiple sclerosis. I'm at a different place today, I know what causes my seizures: It's stress. I had a kind of trauma, if you could call it that. My parents got divorced. I went to live with my dad. It was hard to live with him. Part of having these seizures lies in that history and together with my "I want to be perfect" ideas, I think at one point my body just said "okay it's enough, you cannot do this anymore." I was very, very, very demanding on myself. And sort of surprisingly it was when I was living with my mom and life actually became calm again and I had a normal life again: that is when the seizures appeared.

What do your seizures look like?

At first I didn't lose consciousness, but after a week I did start to lose consciousness. When I have a seizure now I fall on the floor and my body shakes. When I hurt myself it's not that bad but sometimes when I hit the floor it's hard you know. They used to happen a couple of times a day, especially in the gap year that I had when treatment started with my psychologist and last year, my first year in university was also pretty intense because you have to have so many activities and you want to take part but you have to know you cannot do everything at once. Now I have them once a month and even once every two or three months. So it's already a really big progress. It takes me about two to three days to fully recover though. Physically, it's exhausting.

I find that what is most helpful in dealing with my seizures is dealing with them because not thinking about things was what caused me to have seizures, not thinking about my emotions. PNES was really a wake-up call for me to just stand still and answer "how do I feel?" Now I really try to talk about things with friends or my boyfriend.

Since I started having PNES, I have also noticed some changes. I would say that my concentration is a bit less, so it depends on how tired I am. Also before a seizure I get sort of absent minded. They can see my face looks like I'm not there.

How would you describe your family/friends' reactions to your PNES?

It depends. It happened to me on Friday and I was with my colleagues. They had never seen my seizures before and there I was on the floor and when I woke up and I saw these faces above me. It's a bit off putting. It takes some time mentally to recover because you just know that people are really afraid when they see this. But if it happens with my boyfriend or anyone else, they are so used to it so it's different.

My mother's side of the family has been quite helpful. My boyfriend, his parents are really good to me and my mom. My mom is a special person so she's a bit like "ahh!" when something happens. It's stressful but my boyfriend and his parents are really calm and that's what I need sometimes.

My friends try their best to understand it. Of course it's also really hard for them to fully understand. I think sometimes my boyfriend and my really close family don't even understand fully and they're confronted with it every day or weekly or monthly.

How would you describe your quality of life since you've developed PNES?

In the beginning it sucked. I'm not going to lie. You feel not understood and really bad. But I am the kind of person that fights, I fight for myself and I was determined to get out of this. So I made really big changes. Moving out, living on my own while everyone was saying to me "oh you're gonna be lonely and this and that" but I never was and I think those changes also made my quality of life way better because the seizures disappeared. No one can walk into my home now unless I allow them in.

When I have a seizure now sometimes I ask myself "was it worth it? Was it worth what I did this week? I know I'm tired, I know this can happen, but was it worth it?" and if the answer is "yes," then it's fine.

What would you like to tell others in your life, your family, your friends, medical professionals, about what it's like to live with PNES and also what can they do to help you, or really to help anyone deal with this?

Well to my mom I would say "Let me go a bit more."

To the medical profession, I would like to say to them that they should acknowledge psychological conditions more. I think there's much ignorance in the medical field about this and I think it's really a shame because they could gain a lot from learning about it. It's not only PNES, but there's so many people they cannot diagnose simply because they do not look into it more.

What would you say you've learned personally living with PNES?

What I would say about what it's like to live with PNES is different now than four years ago. Now, I would say: it's a part of my life. It's my alarm system for when I am getting too stressed, and I have learned to live with it. I think it's really important to listen to yourself. I think we live in a society where the pressure is on all the time, you have to be on-call all the time, Facebook is there all the time, and I think you really need to take the time to listen to your body because a lot of people don't. PNES is learning how to do it the hard way. I try to take a moment every day where I do some yoga exercises, just 5 or 10 minutes just think about "how do I feel today". I think that's really important because I never did that before.

What are your plans for your future, what do you see in your future?

I have big plans (laughs)! I'm going to do an internship this summer. I can see my future related to PNES or to the conversion disorder umbrella somehow. We live in a society where we have 25 year olds who are already burnouts. We cannot go on like this.

I want to be involved getting these ideas to the public. Policy ideas are great but I want to make them work. For instance, make sure the connection between the medical professionals and psychologists is better because there would be so much to gain from it.
I have been writing a blog on PNES for almost a year. The purpose of it is to share thoughts about PNES but also knowledge. With the blog I notice I run into people that I don't even know that well and they mention "oh I read your blog" and then they know.

I talked with a neurologist here in the Netherlands. He's an epileptologist. He's doing a lot of research and I honestly asked him "what do you think about this idea? Am I too idealistic to want to change this?" and he said "No I don't think you are, I have a lot of patients I diagnose and it would be great if there would be something that could help with that". I also had contact with the epilepsy center that diagnosed me and they are very keen on getting ideas and talking about it once I get back and I also emailed the Dutch Epilepsy Foundation. So, I'm still waiting for answers.

JB or Jerrod
Missouri
Feb 2015

JB is 40 years old. He divorced his wife in 2014 and has no children. He lives alone with his rescue dog. He was granted social security benefits in 2011. Before becoming disabled, he worked as a front desk supervisor in a hotel. He suffered a head injury while in high school and went from taking college prep classes to not being able to continue. He eventually went on to earn a GED.

Diagnostic history
My seizures started at about 35 years of age. At first, in 2010, I would just sort of shut down. I was diagnosed with some form of cataplexy. My doctor also knew that I wasn't sleeping well, so he thought it could be related to that. I had a sleep study and they found out that I had sleep apnea. I saw a neurologist there, and he was "one of the bad kinds," without even looking at my records he said "well I think you need to see a psychiatrist." I went back to my doctor, and he said "we're not putting up with that, I'm going to find you a better doctor." He sent me to Columbia, Missouri to a doctor who was specialized in conversion disorder. When I met him he was very excited because he said I was atypical. They did several studies and that's when I was diagnosed with it. In 2011, the seizures changed. The first one lasted four hours and I broke the recliner that I was in. When my mom called the hospital, they thought it might be an allergic reaction so they suggested she give me Benadryl. When she gave it to me, it worked; it calmed everything down and ever since, when I have a seizure, I take liquid Benadryl. I started having five to six full-on seizures a day where my

entire body twisted up and lurched about. Through a strong antihistamine that is also an anti-anxiety medication, they were able to get it to three to four times a day, which was much better. They also became less violent. Now I tighten up and I twist a little bit but I'm not smacking my head on things.

Do you know why you have these seizures? What has been your understanding of why you have them?

It's a bit of a long story. When my wife and I first got together in about '99 she was alcoholic. Since I had dealt with an alcoholic father growing up, I refused to deal with it, so I kicked her out and then she stopped drinking for me. But that's when the real problems started coming about. She was self-medicating with the alcohol; she had schizophrenia and was bipolar. In 2003 I married her, partly so she would know that I would always be there for her. At first we were able to make it work but eventually as it got worse and worse for her, she couldn't work anymore and eventually it got so bad that I had to stop working so I could take care of her. She needed 24/7 care. Her episodes involved hallucinations, seeing dead people out walking around outside, things in the ceiling, things coming to get her. She would scratch and claw at herself because she thought bugs were on her. And then throughout the night she might get up and try to go out the door and walk down the street. So, I literally never got any rest. We were together for 15 years and it was like this the majority of that. I kept thinking "I can do it, I can do it, I gotta be there for her". But it started wearing down on me physically. I see a cognitive behavioral therapist and I love the way she put it: "our ability to handle stress is like the shell that's around us and whenever things are stressing us out, it's like they're throwing little rocks at our shell and it's chipping away at it." And then when it gets broken down so much you can no longer rebuild. Then every little thing that comes at you, it doesn't matter how small, it's going to hurt just as much as a big stress. And eventually your brain is like "okay, how am I going to deal with all of this?". So that's when it starts converting it to different things.

Were you ever diagnosed with any other disorder? Any other illness before having been diagnosed with PNES?

In '92 I had a head injury as a result of a head-on collision. I was told everything was ok, but I still had trouble (pressure in my head and dizzy spells); I was a wreck. It took 3 years of going to doctors before someone found out that my skull had been shoved into my brain. A lot of doctors just said "oh it's all in your head." Because I had long hair at the time, was 19 and liked to dress in black, I was into metal. They would suggest I was a literally a head-banger and that's why I was having trouble. There was even one doctor that flat out said to my parents "he's just doing this to mooch off of you." That was not very useful. Once the skull issues were finally discovered, we went back to the first MRI people who had originally claimed nothing out of the ordinary, and we said "look at that again." They did and then found there was, in fact, swelling on the brain where the skull pressure was found. They just weren't doing their job the first time. If nothing else, I certainly dealt with a load of stress during that period in addition to the pain of the actual skull pressure. I'm sure it didn't help matters in the future.

What do you find helps you to not have the seizures? Have you noticed anything?

If I don't get enough rest, then my seizures are more frequent. Loud unexpected noises set me off, like a fainting goat. Ever since the accident I've been sensitive to certain things. My friends always kidded me about being a vampire because the bright sun light always hurt my eyes a little more, which I've found to be caused by frequent dilation of my eyes. But if there's a high pitched noise, it will really hurt my ears. It's like my senses were hurt; I think it had something to do with the brain injury. But now, with a loud noise, I'll actually feel pain. It's like I'm getting tasered. And I know this may sound weird but if somebody says something to me that is just incredibly stupid, my whole forehead will literally tense up with extreme pain until I start having a seizure. I think it's an emotional thing because for the longest time, if my wife would give me a kiss, I would drop, as if that feeling of love does me in. Any sudden shift like that, good or bad.

I was getting so bad last summer, dealing with the pain all day, the seizures and then I started getting another symptom to where everything was tasting horrible. Fluids were tasting like gasoline and food would taste like feces. It was just horrible so I stopped eating. My neurologist was moving to another country, and one of the last things he said was "you haven't progressed much in the last 3 years, and it's because your situation hasn't changed. Until your situation at home changes, you're not going to make any progress." I caught what he was saying. I realized I couldn't keep taking care of my wife. She was not getting any better with her condition and I was only getting worse. I had to put her in a mental home. And for her benefits, I had to divorce her. Sure enough, I've gotten a lot better since then. Now I have seizures maybe a couple a week.

What would you say has been your experience with medical professionals as a whole?

I think it's been positive. As for mental health professionals, it's also been ok. I'm actually seeing my ex-wife's psychiatrist now. Only for medication because since my neurologist moved away I need someone to manage my meds. This psychiatrist said, "I know nothing in the field of conversion disorders, I can't help you" but I explained that I'm seeing the cognitive behavioral therapist so really I just needed someone to manage my meds. He agreed. I've been seeing my cognitive behavioral therapist for a year. It took me some time to get started because I felt that this was mainly because of the accident. So it took me a while to really come to terms with the fact that "I can't necessarily handle everything I've been doing with my wife." I kept thinking "I'm tough, I can handle it." It took me a while to finally say "it really is breaking me down and I need help." So that's when I went looking for a cognitive behavioral therapist. The first one I found tried to teach me relaxation techniques but they weren't all that helpful because if a seizure is going to hit me it's sudden. I can't do a relaxation technique prior to a seizure to ward it off. That therapist moved on after a few months, so I ended up finding another one. That's who I'm with now. And she's been wonderful. She seemed to know a lot about conversion disorder. She's the one that explained the whole shell thing to me. Something that helps me now, in the vein of a relaxation technique, is that if I feel something coming on I've gotten better at just making my mind go blank. I realize that part of my problem with the seizure escalating into something severe was I would get stressed saying "uh oh, here it comes" and then that would stress me out more and bring it on stronger. I've taught myself that if something's happening, if I'm starting to go limp or if I get startled, I try to wipe my mind clean to keep stress from building up. Then a lot of times, it will pass.

And as far as outside influences, the worst possible thing is for people to react to my seizures. Because if they start stressing… One problem with my ex-wife was she never could learn to react properly. She would always over-react and so she was causing a lot of my seizures throughout the day. As for the emergency room, they don't respond well either. I've had smelling salts under my nose while I'm fully awake! One time I went to the ER, I was having a cataleptic spell and this nurse came in and started thumping hard in the middle of my chest and then digging in. It hurt, I was awake, but I couldn't move. But the big thing I've found in hospitals is you can try to forewarn them all you want to and it doesn't matter. When you actually have the seizure, it's still a big shock to them because it's something that can go on for 20 minutes or more. They're never prepared. One time I was having scanning on my midsection and they put a dye in my blood. I forewarned them that there was a chance I might have a seizure and sure enough, when they pulled me out, I couldn't move anymore. They started panicking. They thought I'd died on them and they called a code. Luckily they called the emergency doctor and he had seen me the previous night, so he explained "oh he does that, he's okay." Thank goodness for him.

What do you prefer to call your condition?

I usually just call it conversion disorder. Mainly because my neurologist always called it that.

Do you feel that you have the support and understanding of your family, friends?

I feel I do. My mother has tried to learn about this condition. She read a book that came out about PNES. She's been very supportive and right there with me. She doesn't want me to go through what I went through with my head injury again. She said "We're gonna immediately drop any doctor that doesn't seem like he wants to help and only gonna stick with the doctors that do want to help".

I also have a brother who is always there for me if I do need something. And I do have some great friends who are with me and are very supportive. We joke about the conversion disorder. Like if I do something that makes them mad they say "yeah I'm gonna come by your house with an air horn." So we laugh at it. But if I have any problems, they know what to do.

Is there anything that you would like to people in your life about what it's like to live with PNES?

Well that's the thing. I've always been so open with them, all of them know it. I tend to liken what I have to the Hulk, because it's like having the Hulk in you. Not necessarily that you're going to rage out and start destroying things. But if you get too stressed out, it's going to take over your body and it's going to rain hell on you. The Hulk is constantly trying to stay at a balance with his stress and emotional levels because he doesn't want that thing to come out and hurt him or whatever. And once the Hulk is out, the more stress that's around him, the worse it gets. That's how I explain it to someone who just doesn't have a clue.

Would you say you've learned something from having conversion disorder? Has it taught you anything? Has it changed you in any way?

It definitely taught me that even though I'm 6' 2' and have always been a strong, bulky guy and I thought I could handle just about everything, that I worked the best when I was stressed out; it's not true. I learned that there are more ways to break somebody down than just physical and it's just amazing. I know the mind can do strange things and I was so amazed, though terrified, when it first happened. When it first occurred, I kept saying "well there are people fighting wars and going through worse than I am, so does that make me weaker?" But I learned that you can be strong physically and your mind can still break all that down. Even if you have a strong mind and a strong body, if you overload, too much stress can crumble it all. I underestimated its power.

Have you found any side effects from having these seizures?

My memory and concentration is horrible. I'm an author and it's very difficult to do anything with that nowadays, which always troubles me. But, at the same time I've got to keep it from stressing me out, so that's a struggle in itself because the number one thing that I love is reading as well as writing and those abilities are crippled with this. I've got a kindle full of books that I hardly touch because most of the time, I go to read something and my mind goes blank a few paragraphs in. The same goes with writing.

What do you see for your future?

I'm very good at building websites. It's one thing I can do that my lack of concentration doesn't seem to hinder. My motto that I go by is "adapt and conquer." Whenever something happens, don't dwell on what you can't do. Figure out your limits, learn what you can do and then excel at that. That's where I started my site, Balzertown. Through Balzertown, any friends that really need a web presence, I can add them there. I'm calling them "citizens of Balzertown." It's something that gives people smiles. I also still write when I can. I write horror but it usually has dark humor in it. I also know how to make e-books so when I can, I try to help other author friends make their books into e-books, I'm just always trying to be there for people when I can. It all keeps the cabin fever

away because I am stuck at home most of the time. I want to help spread the word any chance I get about conversion disorder. So I pretty much stick with my page and then anyone who wants to talk about it, they're more than welcome to approach me.

ES
New Jersey
February 2015

ES is a 50 year old single woman who has no children. She worked in retail for an extended period of time but was let go after developing her seizures. She is currently unemployed and hoping to find a new job someday soon.

Diagnostic history

I first became aware of the PNES in the September before I was diagnosed. I was diagnosed in December of that same year. I was lucky to be diagnosed so quickly. I really think it was because I was in the right place at the right time with the right doctors available to me. But even with that all I can remember about being told I had PNES was the shock I was in. I do not remember exactly what was said to me but all I heard was that I was crazy. And that what she was telling me was that I was crazy. That was not what the doctor said, but that was what I heard. I really thought I was losing it, so I do not remember too many details. All I was focused on was the fact that in some way I was "doing this to myself" and that it was "under my control". I was worried about how to explain this to friends and family.

The doctor was compassionate. After I broke down, she explained that PNES was not as commonly and openly recognized as it should be. That explanation was definitely something that I held onto when I went to other health care professionals. I quickly realized that many medical professionals were not helpful/understanding when they realized that it was a mental health issue and not a medical issue. Even within the mental health field I found that it was misunderstood. Many of the doctors seemed to be unaware of the condition, and worse, very judgmental. I really felt like I was being looked down upon by those that did not understand PNES. It was almost as though they thought it was not a valid diagnosis and that I was making it up.

That was the most frustrating part....Feeling isolated.

Quality of life

Since I have not had any further episodes since April after the diagnosis I feel that my quality of life has changed but could be a lot worse. I am not worried about the next episode. Through therapy I am able to recognize when I am feeling stressed out and how to deal with it. I also feel that the treatment that I received was helpful in explaining the diagnosis. I know that trauma was what caused the seizures to start and once I recognized that was the cause I was able to work on treating the trauma in therapy. That helps me to "control" the seizures. I am able to identify when I am feeing stressed out or depressed and can use that to help me manage my mood and my PNES.

Treatment from Friends/Family

Since the diagnosis and the treatment I still think that my friends and family misunderstand the diagnosis. Maybe they do not fully understand the diagnosis. They try to do research and what they find is very negative and makes them feel worse about it. They are trying to support me but I do not think that they have the tools to help me. I wish there was more material out there that they can read. There really is not much information out there for friends and family.

At my job, after I went out on disability after the first couple of episodes, and returned to the job I was treated very poorly and ultimately was fired due to poor work performance. But I think that is what they were using as an excuse but really it was related to the PNES and going out on disability. Currently I am not working and I am thinking about getting back to work shortly. I am physically able to work but have not had the motivation to put myself back into the work world yet.

To the medical professionals

All I would want to say is: treat us like you would treat any other patients. We are not second class citizens. We want help just like anyone else. We are not doing this on purpose or for attention. It is your responsibility to be more aware and up to date on these types of conditions and if you don't know about it then at least research it before being dismissive.

Take Away

If I take anything away from this whole experience it is that I was truly lucky that I was at the right place at the right time. If I had not been treated by the medical professional I saw the first time I went to the ER, I do not know what would have happened. I am afraid that I would have been misdiagnosed and not received the treatment that I needed.

*The only way to
get better
is to
surround
yourself with
people
who believe in you.*

KR
February 2015
England

KR is 50 years old, single and has no children. She lives in the south of England in a Georgian market town, close to the sea and New Forest. She has a diagnosis of PNES and PTSD and currently does voluntary work in a charity shop doing window displays. (KR chose to participate in this book project responding in writing rather than through a phone interview).

I first became unwell in May 2010.

My Philosophy Today

I try to live my day in the moment. I try not to look ahead to the future, whilst allowing my past to flow in and out. I catch myself, and don't feed those unhelpful thoughts and allow them to grow bigger and out of control. A bad morning does not mean a bad afternoon or a bad following hour. I take time to look at things, absorb them, which in this fast technological world isn't a bad thing. It takes work, but this is how I live. In the moment.

I have learned to say 'no' and not do what makes me uncomfortable. If I don't want to do something, or say yes when I mean no and just trying to 'please'. My body tells me I am not being truthful to myself. I may get a head twitch -like waving a massive flag on top of my head saying "NO SHE DOES NOT LIKE WHAT YOU ARE SAYING"! As a born people pleaser this was not easy but now it really is. If I am stressed or uncomfortable I can't hide it. "No" comes a lot easier theses days and really makes life easier.

My saving grace and what has kept me sane all this time is my creativity. One day I went to the library and picked up a book on making sock toys. This has led to a whole World of creativity. Those times I am bed bound, those times I have racing thoughts, I direct them to my latest project. Being bored or unable to do much actually is a useful tool for me as it can allow ideas to come in and out and flow. For me, this is my meditation, it keeps me grounded and focused.

It may be useful to give some information on the variety of difficulties, which the condition presents. On my part, they have changed over time and some may be present at times, ease off or disappear and another one appears/reappears. The one constant is seizures, although their form may vary, vocal tics, and twitches coupled with hyper arousal. Following this I will give various positives, which may help ease or benefit another person, which I have tried.

SEIZURES, HYPER AROUSAL, TWISTING OF FACE (LOOKED LIKE I HAD A STROKE) AVOIDANCE, FLASHBACKS, INTRUSIVE THOUGHTS, NIGHTMARES, HALLUCINATIONS, SPASMS THROUGHOUT BY BODY, STAMMER, POOR GAIT, FALLING DOWN, FATIGUE, WORD FINDING DIFFICULTIES, POOR CONCENTRATION, PROBLEMS SLEEPING, LOSS OF SPEECH, SLURRED SPEECH, VOCAL TICS, BODY TICS AND JERKS, SEVERE STOMACH CRAMPS, SWALLOWING DIFFICULTIES, DIZZINESS, BACK AND NECK PAIN, LOSS OF APPETITE, ANXIETY, ARM RAISING IN THE AIR, TRANCES, CLAUSTROPHOBIA, OVER EATING, BREATHING DIFFICULTIES, MEMORY PROBLEMS, EYES CLOSING SHUT, SENSORY ISSUES. Probably more, but I think this is enough to mention.

Back and neck. I use a heated wheat bag, popped in the microwave and this helps give some comfort to my neck. I have a Pilates roll, which has been such a relief for my back as it helps massage the pumped up muscles and helps align my back. I may use it 2-3 times a day when particularly uncomfortable.

Racing thoughts. In the past I have used a grounding technique, which involves moving or looking around the room looking at objects and describing them out loud. "This is a white china cup, it feels hard and cold". You could carry something in your pocket to feel and describe to yourself. A string of beads of various shapes and sizes is good and you feel each bead individually and describe it to yourself. This technique can on occasions help when you are in a situation where you feel a seizure is likely, to redirect your attention.

Spasms in throat and neck. Yawning, moving your jaw from side to side, laughing or, opening your mouth slightly and dropping your tongue to the bottom of your mouth can be a relief. I picked this up in speech therapy.

Getting to sleep. I do take a mild sleeping tablet Zopiclone 3.75mg each night. However, I find if I do a simple book of mixed puzzles when in bed, I always get to the point where I am tired I usually drop the book and pen and am asleep quickly. This has over time helped me greatly with my word finding difficulties and there is a little sense of achievement. If I have a particular thought that is lingering I will tell myself out loud to 'stop it' and 'don't make it bigger'. If I can't sleep and am restless I will get up, go to the lounge, something to eat and drink and put on the television until I am tired. I may fall asleep on the couch but that's ok. Sleep is important. Very important.

Concentration. This was really tricky and still can be a challenge. I could not read more than a couple of lines initially. The concentration in absorbing what I was reading proved too much. I got a newspaper and would pick out very small articles and, when I achieved my target of reading it, I would cross it out. I would have the newspaper for days. I remember having crossed off nearly every article on one paper after two weeks – but I had done it! After 5 years, I have just completed reading a whole book, which was in small manageable sections.

Exhaustion. All you can do is rest. Stop everything and ride it out. I often get up in the morning, have my breakfast and end up having to go to bed for another hour. Maybe you will have to do this; maybe you will have unpleasant sensations in your body, like a rush of adrenaline or anxiety. Ride it out. Maybe, after a period of time you will be able to get up and do something. Put that time in bed behind you, you can't change it. It happened, maybe the next hour or more will be better. Often it can be.

Goals. Setting a goal should be achievable and simple in the early days. I remember setting myself tasks such as washing my hair or buying flowers or making a phone call. Also, if I did not meet the goal, I did not beat myself up about it. Sometimes I achieved it a week later. So what? I achieved it. It is hard, it is frustrating, those feelings are warranted and you are allowed to feel them. But, one foot in front of the other – ok? I found music intolerable unless, strangely, it was classical or opera. I think it may be the base or rhythm. However in year 4, I booked to go and see Madame Butterfly some months ahead. My health dictated at that time I could not go. It was a real shame. This year (2015) I have been to the ballet to see Swan Lake. I went with a friend, armed with my ear-plugs, ear defenders (bright pink) and a small cushion. I made it, left wobbling up the aisle as the applause started and the attendant let us out a side door. It just needed a good day and a little preparation. I have booked ahead to see various other events at the theatre throughout the year. I hope to go but I am also realistic that there is a chance on that day it won't be possible. Fingers crossed!

Isolation. This is hard. We have an unseen, misunderstood condition that the medical profession does not have a handle on. The word Mental Illness throws up all sorts of connotations for people. How do we even accept it? I could not accept for years that it was a psychological condition. I remember my mother saying 'why are you seeing a psychiatrist, you aren't mad?" I really struggled/struggle with the rejection, abandonment and false promises I have received from people I had previously believed cared about me. Some people who worked in the care field with me for years could apparently 'not cope'. I have had someone cross the road to avoid me. I have had someone walk a few steps away with their back to me when I am on a pavement with my hands banging on the ground. I have had someone offer to walk to the park with me with his children and left me gripping on to a wire fence in a seizure, whilst he walked away and did not so much as ring me later to see how I was. I sadly have no answer to this. I don't understand. Interestingly some people I have met who did not know me for years before my PNES/PTSD have welcomed me into their lives. I am grateful for them. However, I have been fortunate to have a couple of friends who have picked me up off the floor, made me food, and been there for me.

Keep a Journal. After a couple of years I decided to keep a daily journal. This was useful in that it allowed me to express how I felt, what I did in the day, how may seizures I had. It served as a record, a marker of my mood, things I had enjoyed and showed that every hour of every day was not marked by my condition. I would write down small things, like the sun was out, someone had rung me. It has served as a release, record for the medical profession and myself. If I had a particularly unwell day I may just write 'lots of fits' if I lost count. I do remember a time writing that my seizures had reduced, during one month, to over 90. Another month to in the 70's. It could be looked at later to show both improvements, achievements, dips, changing signs and symptoms and my thoughts and feelings and environmental influences. It is worth doing.

I would like to tell people that this is debilitating, I am doing the best I can. Before PNES I would travel the World on my own, was spontaneous, creative with plans for my life. My intention had been to move to Italy. I may not always be in control of my body but my mind is fully functional. My brother always told any medical bodies or agencies, 'watch it, she is bright as a button'. If you talk and talk and talk I will ask you to slow down or stop for a minute. I am the same personality and have all the characteristics I always did. Don't patronize me. When I have a seizure I can hear everything you say and know where you are in the room and am fully aware, even when I am paralyzed and unable to communicate. Be tolerant. Even if you don't understand because you can't see a broken limb, accept I have a little understood condition and believe and accept me. No, I don't ever put it on for attention, to gain something, or avoid something. Maybe you are uncomfortable around me but this is short lived. I don't have the luxury of avoiding myself.

Background

In 2007 having left a 9 year relationship, my job as a team manager working with boys with a diagnosis of Aspergers Syndrome, I was exhausted, depressed and went to live in Alexandria in Egypt to 'escape' reality and attempt to live a peaceful life. I had had nothing left to give, had worked myself into the ground in an environment where by the very nature of the job you needed to keep an element of calm, dampening down your emotions and feelings to not to react to the physical and emotional occurrences which were encountered on a daily basis. I cared deeply for the students and was passionate about doing the best for them and my team. Unfortunately there was not in place, as in many such care environments, to have a debrief and, getting home sometimes at gone midnight did not allow the body to unwind and I often went to bed with my mind racing, planning and adrenaline still surging through my body. I was able to eloquently describe my feelings and emotions but as yet unable to know how to deal with these and work through them. My partner, a gentle kind man began also working shifts. We did not have a relationship as time went by – he choosing solitary past times, surfing, biking and I turned more into myself with nothing left to give to him or myself. Also I wanted children and marriage and he didn't at this point in our relationship.

I had the previous year gone to Egypt for 3 months to fulfill a hope, of helping children and gave up my job, sold my car, raised some money to help street children with an NGO in Alexandria. I ended up working in the desert and slum areas taking resources and doing some work with the children. I spoke only a couple of words but with movement and enthusiasm it worked. At the time of my depression in 2007, it was suggested I go back to Egypt. Impulsive. Always been impulsive. It was like someone had switched a light on and all my energy went into leaving. I was actually very unwell, had been to the doctor with suicidal thoughts. I left England and moved to Egypt, where I entered into a relationship with an Egyptian man, who potentially offered me all I thought I wanted at that time. He turned out to be a controlling and psychologically and at times physically abusive. I managed to get out of this relationship after some time but had felt unsafe, had my home broken into, my car broken into. I turned to another man for help. I was again very unwell and broken. Breaking my relationship with my long-term partner had caused ripples with my family and I felt I could not return to the UK and needed to stay as I had made my bed. This new man was a worse choice. More psychologically abusive and terrorized me. I felt like a psychological hostage. He was obsessed with me. I was afraid for my life.

The start of PNES

I had for years, when tired, had little jerks as some people do, meaning 'go to bed'. These were only when late at night but had started during the daytime. They increased in intensity when tired in the evening. When in Egypt I saw a doctor and he gave me a tablet and this stopped. At the time I was working in an international British school as a teacher in a nursery class traveling an hour to work which increased to 1.5 hours through noisy, dug up roads, constant honking of horns, heat, polluted areas and into a classroom of beautiful but typically noisy 3 year old children. Next to my ground floor flat at home, was a café. The café was undergoing renovation work. This involved starting before 8am and going on until midnight. It was so loud I could not hear my television sometimes. I would bury my head in cushions and cry. I could not escape noise. It felt like torture. On top of that I had rescued a street cat that became pregnant and her 5 kittens would wake early and bang my bedroom door. I cried a lot. I felt trapped with nowhere to go and nobody to trust. The jerks became more frequent and I sought help from a doctor again. In his surgery my body started jerking. They sent me to a psychologist, then the top neurologist in Alexandria. During an EEG my body went into a full seizure. I was terrified. He told me I had myoclonic epilepsy. He prescribed me Xanax and a pill for epilepsy. I became worse. My body going limp, difficulty walking, seizures, strange laughing. I had a brain scan, blood taken until I ended up in hospital, where they said they could do nothing for me. My younger brother was called and returned me to the UK.

UK medical treatment

I lived with my brother and at this time was having about 12-15 seizures a day, lasting 20 minutes or more. Noise sensitive, even the stirring of a spoon in a cup of teas was unbearable. I was hunched over, my legs turned slightly inward and I shuffled when I walked. No appetite and the noise of some foods, e.g. crisps, seemed to resonate loudly in my head. After one week back in the UK and an episode of struggling to breathe, I was admitted to hospital in Brighton, East Sussex. I was there for 2 weeks. I had various tests and was monitored for pupil dilation, length of seizure. Every time I had my blood pressure taken, I had a seizure. Finally, I was visited by a consultant, and told that I did not have epilepsy and to stop the medication. I was not given any information that it was psychological cause but said I would be transferred to a neurological unit. This filled me with more fear. It was not explained to me what was wrong. Some nurses were sympathetic and kind. Some left me feeling like I was a nuisance and on one occasion, was banging my head against the bars on the bed in a seizure and told to "stop it". Another time was 3am; I could not sleep, I had been fitting off and on and was exhausted. This final seizure was 45 minutes. At this stage of my illness, my arms would violently thrash, my head move back as my back arched. I would stare, wide eyed in a fixed position, usually up to the right of the wall/ceiling. The male nurse was staring out of the window, tapping his pen and when I finally stopped. I begged him for a sleeping tablet. He said he could not give me one and told me to 'go to sleep', and walked away. I felt humiliated, afraid and lay crying to myself. Exhausted, I was awoken by a nurse about 7am telling me to take a tablet. My hair was matted, I was wet from sweat and I physically could not swallow. I was lying flat and she tried to get me to swallow the tablet. I was moved that day unwashed, covered in sweat. The process was hurried and they were unprepared with the paperwork. The journey in ambulance was difficult as I was fitting badly and it was long. They were kind. At the neurological unit, the level of noise was torture. My brother was on his way and I did not want him to see the mess physically I was in so I desperately brushed my matted hair. I was due to have another EEG with a video. My brother was forceful that I needed a side room. I could not stop fitting. Eventually I did get a side room, and earplugs. The beep of machines, talking, laughing, general noise was intolerable. I remember a visitor to one of the patients had a crisp packet. I curled up in the corner of the room under the covers, with a pillow over my head. I had to request they stop taking my blood pressure. I felt like a nuisance. I remember hearing a nurse and trainee nurse talking during one seizure one was tapping her pen and sighed heavily having read they usually lasted for 25 minutes. I had asked my brother to write for the staff, any information I felt could be useful, Duration, I could hear, needed quiet, which none of them it transpired had read. I was meant to have physio and was collected by them in a wheelchair. As we went down a corridor I was aware of a lot of noise ahead and was concerned about this and told them I was going to have a seizure. I was told that I 'was not'. I did. My head flopped back over the back of the chair as I thrashed and became more uncomfortable. Nobody moved to help me. They talked amongst each other. I again felt humiliated and afraid. I was prescribed during my time at the neurological unit 7.5mg of sleeping tablet Zopiclone each night. After 2 weeks I was discharged to the care of my brother in Brighton, to be referred to a psychologist. I had not received any physiotherapy but was sent home with a leaflet.

Out of hospital

Going in the sun for more than 10 minutes caused a seizure. My arms started jerking and raising in the air and round in circles. I was unable to read, my concentration was so poor, and I would repeat the same sentence tying to remember or take in what I read. My hands turned inwards. My body hurt. One night the pain in my stomach was so bad I crawled on my hands and knees to outside my brother's bedroom but the fear of returning to hospital prevented me from knocking on his door. We bought a wheelchair. I was housebound. My brother went through the mechanics of walking with me as I had forgotten how to move my hips, knees: the mechanics of walking. It was a Forest Gump moment! He arranged for me to visit an osteopath he knew well. It was a light bulb moment. This man talked to me about the different nervous systems, and the effects of stress/trauma have. At my brother's home I researched and discovered PNES. The osteopath did some research himself. He cared and suggested a mild acupuncture in my legs. At this visit I was open to trying this, felt safe, and calm. He put one fine needle in my knee. It did not hurt and I felt fine. Very quickly things changed. My arms violently flapped forwards on the couch and then over my head, thrashing rapidly forwards and backwards. I was terrified. It was like some kind of possession. I was crying. The seizures for the next 6 months took on this vein, and were so physically demanding I lost nearly 2 stone.

Psychological help

After 6 months, I moved out of living with my brother to a rented room about 2 miles away. I felt he was unable to cope and had gone into a shut down. For the sake of our relationship I left. I was trying to not be in the way, not a nuisance, and started to develop OCD in obsessing about washing up. I have never been this way inclined and was aware of it. I caught it quickly. I could not control my body my surroundings and felt a burden. I had needed to control something.

I was referred to a psychologist – female – at my request. I had a fear of men. There had been an attempted rape in Egypt and a doctor out there had molested me. Coupled with the abuse and control I received, I am still to this day uncomfortable in 1:1 situations in male company with few exceptions. She was ineffective. She did not make notes and I would give her information (from my background in care work), which I knew were worthwhile: how many seizures, what I was doing at the time, triggers, duration etc. The journey to see her was over an hour in a car. I would fit in the car, outside the waiting room and in her room. On two occasions she was not there and had failed to let me know. One time I was fitting on and L-shaped corridor, nobody helped me, stopped to ask if I needed help. I dropped my bag and was aware of someone looking at me and leaving. I had also dropped my water. It was an assistant who I saw, and about whom I made a complaint later as her language and questioning were wholly inappropriate and insulting. The psychologist called in a psychiatrist, as my body jerks were so difficult and uncontrollable. I had to tie my right arm down in my coat belt if I went out. He said it was a case of suppression like Freud's Hysteria and prescribed Mertazepine. He was with me no more than 5-10 minutes. I felt angry and not listened to. I took half the prescribed Mertazepine and was so unsteady I nearly fell down the stairs. I had taken the tablet in the morning and by 5pm called my brother to help. He said my pupils were huge. I did not take this tablet again. Six months later I woke and my face on the left side was twisted looking like I had had a stroke. I could barely speak. I had previously had an episode of loss of speech whereby any attempt to speak would result in my throat going into spasm proving difficult to breathe. The facial twist remained with me for over 3 years.

The short-term room rental came to an end and I moved to rent a room in the New Forest in Hampshire where I had lived for some time previously. Hoping that being with familiar surroundings and some people I knew, I continued to have phone counseling with the lady clinical psychologist in Brighton. One time she said she really wanted me to come to Brighton to see her. I went up the day before; I had 8 seizures getting there by train. It took me 2hours 45 minutes to get there. I had a call the morning of the appointment from her secretary to say sorry she was not well. Some days later she talked to me about discontinuing therapy with her. I felt let down. I did not consider her a suitable match for me but had felt disinclined to say so due to the fact this was the only 'help' I was receiving. Nobody seemed to have any knowledge or be taking notice of what I was saying. I had felt there was a correlation between the levels of noise I was subjected to in Egypt over a prolonged period and the extreme difficulties I was experiencing with noise currently. During the conversation I began repeating the same few words over and over 'oh dear, oh dear, oh dear...' From this point I developed vocal tics, which I have 5 years later together with word finding difficulties and slight intermittent stammer.

I registered with a doctor locally who was dumbfounded, had never come across this condition before. He referred me to a neurologist and put my name down for a local psychologist. I had lost 2s-tone and my body was wiry from the exhausting seizures. The neurologist had asked if I had been an athlete as I was so toned. He did all the necessary tests and nothing showed up. After some time, at my request I saw a speech therapist. My speech was poor, and labored and I was unable to pronounce various sounds 'the' and 'thing' (would come out as va fing). My word finding usually started with 'va fing wot you call...." And try to describe the word. I sounded foreign with an 'a' added to a lot of words.

Through the National Health Service I was finally allocated a Clinical Psychologist, who I saw for 3 years. My therapy finished at the end of 2014. I still have some difficulties, and places in my head I do not want to visit but most importantly I accept my condition and do the best I can, which is all we can do.

Seizures and other things!

I thankfully don't know what I look like when I have a seizure or pull faces (thank goodness) but can describe how it feels to me.

I have a warning. A little head rush or light-headedness. Time to get myself safe from hurting myself. I am fully conscious. I know where I am and can hear everything. These days my eyes close. Both arms strongly slam down together. Previously up until a couple of months ago my right arm was the dominant. Initially, in the early days my right arm would be up in the air, or moving a lot and particularly to any music with a beat. My left arm was more ballerina-like and graceful and only came out to more genteel music like opera! I called them George and Mildred. Now, with both arms I can tone up nicely for summer! After the thrashing I am exhausted and sometimes feel paralyzed. I may stare and have one arm raised or lay motionless. I can get out of it easier if there is quiet. If people stand over me or lean over me this exacerbates it. When particularly bad, being covered to block all senses can help. Often I feel very cold afterwards. Previously I would shiver. They can last 5-15 minutes depending on the stimulation, environment and activity I have been doing. Recovery time again can vary. Sometimes I can recover after a few minutes. Others, my recover is longer, I am unsteady and vision not blurred but I struggle to keep my eyes open. When a bad seizure happens I will go to bed for a few hours. If I don't get the timing right when recovering, I will lapse into more seizures. When particularly exhausted it may result in 1-3 days in the house, resting. Then starting slowly again. Sometimes, doing something worthwhile and fulfilling may result in a long period of rest, but I would rather experience something than not!

Tip

I have only recently discovered that if someone is around to help, they put cushioning under my arms quite deep (i.e. 2 cushions height), this dampens out the arm flapping somewhat since the movement of the arms is limited. Previously anything soft would be used to protect my arms and head. I did have an awful stage of being prone, in an episode, to slapping myself hard in the face.

Naturally this was distressing but, warning people in advance helped in being prepared and limits getting hurt. I tell people not to get too close to my arms having blackened my poor mother's eye! I have tried reciting poems or counting backwards during seizures but for me, this lengthens the whole thing so I find that not resisting in any way, allowing it to happen and end is the best way.

Vocal tics

I have no thought that I am aware of, in my head prior to the vocal tics. Fortunately I only have 2 words, which are offensive 'cow' and 'pube'. But have had two occasions when I have said 'snap your penis' and loudly said 'vagina' at my mother. I am mortified when this happens. Generally they come about when I am tired, or over stimulated, traveling in a car, too many people talking around me or really concentrating on something or really excited. They always happen when I am working in the charity shop, which is why I don't serve the public on the till, coupled with the fact the beeping of the till, concentration involved would at this stage in my life be too challenging for my body to undertake. Currently, the tics often repeated are: couch, tool, old, mould, old, cow, tubaloo, , holey moley, and sometimes and slightly manic sounding laugh, a whistle, a raspberry, a forceful 'move'. Sometimes it is really funny but, when it goes on for long periods it isn't and is exhausting and can be upsetting. I don't like it. I do use humor a lot and in some ways this gets me through. However, I am aware that I do use it as a mask to avoid vulnerability. The tic apart from being vocal, is accompanied by a contracting of my stomach muscles and spasm in my neck and throat so is physically demanding too. If I can remove myself from the situation or ask people to be quiet I do so. When they are too bad and I am spent and tired, I will reduce all stimulation and go to bed to let the sensations flow out and my body to recover. The energy expended and the fatigue I feel after a long bout of tics is not dissimilar to having a seizure.

Sensory Issues

Noise. I am not convinced in all cases the noise effects me but more like the vibrations of noise. It is like being in a disco and standing next to the speakers with the volume turned down. You can FEEL it. It is uncomfortable. It causes sensations in my body. Imagine a room full of tiny polystyrene balls all floating around. Suddenly they all rapidly move and press against you. That is what I mean by vibration of noise. A noise like an alarm, buzzer, drill, will instantly lead to a seizure. Previously it could be the tap of a keyboard was intolerable. This particular sensory issue has caused me to move twice.

Movement. I am sensitive to rapid movement. A child running by. In a car, when the car is in idle mode, such as a queue or traffic light. I will have a lot of vocal tics and a seizure. If I am in a conversation with more than one person. I get to a point when I can't cope, and need to ask them to stop. It feels like that vibration of noise is too much. It can happen 1:1 also. I cannot cope in a queue. I think my body had become claustrophobic in a way. In the street, I find it hard to stop and talk for too long as the movement of people passing by makes me unsteady. Traveling in a car I find extremely hard as when the car is in idle mode (at traffic lights, in a queue) the movement or vibration will result in a series of vocal tics, jerks and seizure. Usually when the car is stopped to park, I need time to recover before getting out.

Touch. I was unable to receive a hug for nearly 3 years. My mother's dog could be on my lap for 3 seconds maximum. It created a strong reaction in me. My mother always remembers trying to hug me and I pushed her away and screamed. It is like an electric shock. Imagine the smelliest, repulsive person approaches you rapidly and grabs you in the crotch. It is that knee-jerk instant impulse to get away from that touch. We all have personal space. I can now on a good day have a hug and my mother's new dog can sit on me and we can share a much-needed cuddle. We all need the comfort of touch and, since I am extremely tactile, this was particularly isolating, challenging for me, and the cause of much sadness. I used to hold my own hand to get some comfort.

Life these days

I am an optimist. Living in the moment. I use humor to deflect and take away the difficulties. Sometimes, it really is hilarious though. I use a walking stick to help me get around. It also gives people a useful warning and a double decker bus has stopped to let me across the street and a train waited extra 3 minutes for me to get on! My life is very small and limited and although I am alone a lot, I am not often lonely. This has taken years to adjust to and I was lonely for a long time. I am lonely when I have a period of time housebound and unable to do little. Yes, sometimes I cry, but in life we all cry. I have trained myself not to let myself be consumed with a thought. Last year was worse than anything I could have imagined. My father died following a stroke and a 2-year battle with ill health. On the same day mother had a major heart operation, 2 days later I had to have her dog put down. This is partly why live in the right now.

My life is a triangle. I go from a wonderful rented ground floor flat with a walled cottage garden and the wild birds I love. From there I go to a café in a hotel, where the staff know me and get my order as soon as I walk in the door. From there I potter to a Marie Curie charity shop where I volunteer on an 'any time I like' basis; whether it be for a cup of tea and company, to an hour to 3 hours. In these places, the people are warm, accepting. Actually I don't think there is a shop in the town I haven't had a seizure in and I am accepted. I carry a card with me, saying my name, not to call an ambulance, not to touch me but protect my hands etc. Of course some people who have had first aid training will feel the need to put it into use! The intention is good often, but there is often a desire from people to hold my hands to stop me hurting myself and call an ambulance.

  As I write this in my café, the fire alarm goes off and the inevitable happens. Arm toning! My hands are pushed down and held. I manage to free them and mumble. A reassuring voice from the Manager to say all is ok and she will be with me in a minute. No fuss. A glass of water. Understanding. That is just what is needed. My arms ache and my thighs are stinging. My lower back is a bit tight. Time to stop. Time to go home and rest up a little – then carry on. I always carry on.

Seizures today: 4
Tics   : Lots
Smiles   : Too many to mention.

OL
March 2015
Hawaii

OL is a 35 year old, single woman who has no children. She has a Master's in Education, with a specialization in science. She recently completed the Oahu Master Gardener course in Hawaii. She is a science educator and garden teacher, having worked in private child care, the public school setting, and most recently, a farm.

Diagnostic History: The seizures began in January 2007 but I was not formally diagnosed with PNES until 2008. I did not begin treatment for PNES until almost 5 years later when my neurologist at that time recommended a neuropsychologist who treats patients with PNES.

What are your seizures like?
I have two different kinds of episodes, the full body convulsions and the tremors. They often begin with a blank stare followed by stuttering, and movement in one of my arms. Sometimes they progress to full body convulsions. Although I am conscious during these episodes, I am unresponsive. It takes time to recover, sometimes up to 45 minutes, and I am often very tired after.

What was your quality of life when the PNES first started and now?
When I was first diagnosed, there was a huge loss of independence. I was no longer permitted to drive a car. The seizures also affected my employment and annual income. I lost two jobs because of the seizures. In my first job, I was the assistant director of a childcare center with children ranging in age from 6 weeks to 6 years old. The company felt that if there was an emergency at the childcare center and I was incapacitated, I would not be able to carry out my responsibilities which could represent a real danger to myself and the children. When the company let me go because my

medical leave expired, I was okay with this decision because I felt maybe it was not safe, given my seizure condition, for me to supervise young children. I felt that with my second job however, my termination was a result of disability discrimination and medical leave retaliation. I worked as a middle school science teacher and my annual ratings and observations were satisfactory up until I began having a seizure flare-up. I was terminated because, according to the principal, I "did not show adequate impact on student learning." The principal had expressed concern that I would continue having seizure flare-ups and disrupt the students' education and become a financial burden to the school. I sued this employer for disability discrimination and medical leave retaliation and we agreed to a settlement.

This condition took a toll on my social life. I did not like going out and disrupting the good times of my loved ones. I lived in fear of getting hurt and becoming a liability for others but then after some time of living this way, I made a choice. I said to myself, "I'm going to do what I can do to make myself better. I am going to get better." I had this vision, this deep knowingness, that I would get better and that I would be able to help others. And that pushed me to move instead of staying stuck living in fear. My quality of life has improved significantly over the past several years.

One thing I still have dreams of is returning to competing in triathlons. In 2007, the same year I was first began experiencing seizures, I competed in my fourth sprint distance triathlon. I said to myself "these seizures are not going to define me. I'm still going to do what I want to do." After safely completing this triathlon, I began training for an Olympic distance triathlon but during training, I had two seizures, one almost in the pool, and my coach decided it was not safe for me to train with them at that time.

What do you think exacerbates your seizures?
Exhaustion, not getting enough sleep, that is definitely a trigger. Chronic pain, or acute pain is also a trigger. The combination of

not sleeping well enough and not eating well (i.e. eating a lot of processed foods) lowers my seizure threshold. I stay away from artificial sweeteners because I find that they give me tremors. When I go to the dentist, I have special anesthesia-one that does not affect my heart rate as a sudden change in heart rate can also trigger tremors and possibly a convulsion.

What helps you cope with your seizures in a better way

Sleeping, definitely. I was often sleep deprived before. Holistic therapies that include meditation, yoga, acupuncture, and grounding techniques have been essential to my recovery. Changing my eating habits and losing weight was another important part of my recovery. Soon after my diagnosis of PNES, my doctor ran blood tests and found that I was pre-diabetic and said I would surely have diabetes in the near future if I did not take care of it. He referred me to a nutritionist on staff and together we created a food plan to level out my blood glucose levels. I became more conscious of what I was eating. My eating hasn't always been perfect but I have definitely become aware of how food choices impact my health and am mindful of my eating habits. I keep away from the sugar free sweeteners, avoid consuming too much caffeine, and make it a priority to eat fresh, whole foods. I have lost 50 pounds and feel so much lighter and healthier.

Practicing yoga has been an integral part of my recovery. Often when we have seizures, there is a "disconnect" from our physical bodies. Yoga helps us connect to our breath and helps us focus. There is real healing in restoring the mind/body connection. I also think that our bodies store emotions and certain yoga poses help us heal from/release these emotions.

I have continued to see a psychotherapist here in Hawaii as part of my treatment for PNES. I have been working with her for 6 or 7 months now. We do something called "quantum transformational healing" which includes inner child healing. I enter a deep, meditative state. We ask what I need and then we pray for the highest form of healing. I have had seizures in her office during therapy, but I have always felt lighter and better after.

What was your health like before being diagnosed with PNES?

Generally, I was in good physical health although I was overweight and had occasional back pain and high cholesterol.

Do you feel like you have the understanding, the support of your friends there where you're living?

Absolutely. The support I receive from my family and friends has been an important part of my recovery. I am so very grateful to them. They have been amazing. My current supervisor knows of my seizures and has been very understanding. I remember during the interview, purposefully not mentioning anything about the seizures. However, once I was hired, I gave him the letter from my doctor and his response was, "Yes, yes I know. It's going to be fine." Apparently, he already knew of my seizures because he had read my blog prior to my interview. I was very grateful. At work, they are understanding when I need to take breaks. They have been very supportive. As for my family, they have been by my side when I have actually had episodes and have kept me safe. They took me to my doctors' appointments and visited me at the hospital. They spoke with me and encouraged me. I had an aunt who also gave me a place to live when I lost my job.

I have to say though that they have been supportive even though they do not really understand what PNES is. A lot of the older generation relatives thought that I was getting the seizures because I was not married and did not have children. My dad said "if you were to get married and have kids I bet you this would stop."

Maybe they thought that I needed something to "distract me." Maybe the rationale is that when you're thinking about somebody else and what their needs are, the focus is not solely on you so then you will not have seizures. I don't really talk to them about it now. They focus more on physical symptoms so my mom will ask "are you getting enough rest? Make sure you're getting enough rest." With the younger generation, their main thing is keeping me safe. They joke about it too "watch out with her, she'll start shaking like a fish out of water." I feel accepted because everybody's got their something right? That's how it is in my family, everybody's got their something. I've never had anyone say "I don't want to hang out with you because you get seizures". In fact, early on it was I who did not want to socialize because I felt like a burden to others.

Is there anything you would like to tell your family, your friends and other people in your life about PNES?

First I would say a heartfelt thank you to my family and express my gratitude for their love and support because I would not be where I am in my recovery without them.

I also want to say that there is hope for treatment. I've gotten much better and I would like for them not to worry so much. I understand that when a family member has this type of illness where they can get hurt, it's natural to worry a lot. But I want to tell them, my mom especially, to not worry, that it's going to be okay and that I do take care of myself. And for my other family members I would say that it's a condition and that there is hope for healing.

To the doctors, I would say that it is important to be supportive of the person who has PNES and to become knowledgeable about the condition. It's really important to not just see us as a diagnosis but to treat us with respect and dignity because we are people. It's not all in our head. We want to get better. Fortunately, there is a growing network of professionals who understand this.

I would say to those who have been told they have PNES, this diagnosis is not the end of your life. Believe in your body's natural healing abilities. Even though you may not see yourself improving immediately or if you still have the occasional seizure, do not despair and continue to feed your faith-believing that you will improve. Healing is a process. It is your unique journey. Most times, it's not going to happen overnight but if you set your intentions for healing, you will find the support you need to recover.

Do you feel that you've learned anything particular anything personally from having PNES?

Absolutely! And I write about that in my blog. PNES has taught me to pay a lot more attention to how I am feeling, to the signals my body is sending out, to take care of myself, and to make my health and well-being a priority so I can help myself and others. I used to push myself really hard, but I have learned that with PNES, rest is very important. I can't do it all alone and am conscious of asking for help when I need it.

This diagnosis has also put me in touch with my Inner Healer, the Divine Energy. We are whole and our true selves must be seen as whole, healthy, and complete. PNES has also shown me that I am resilient. I remember one of my doctors early on, perhaps because she was thinking about my safety and the safety of others, recommend "for right now you should be working in a back office, filing or something like that, away from people." I did not want to accept that because in my heart, I knew that type of work was not for me. And now here I am, several years later, working on a farm, interacting with children and families on a daily basis. A PNES diagnosis does not mean I have to give up on my dreams. In fact, often you discover in these circumstances, your inner self and the power within. I have discovered my voice again and found a network of support. It has definitely helped me exercise my faith and overcome limitations. This experience of having PNES has drawn me closer to the Universal Life Force, which many call God.

What do you see in your future?

Short term, I am planning on attending a friend's wedding in India then going back to El Salvador to visit my grandparents. I also see myself traveling to different places in the world and perhaps teaching abroad. I hope to live and work on a farm as an educator, taking care of the animals and growing vegetables, and sharing this experience with children. I definitely see this in my future and I also see myself in the next couple of years starting a family- whether it is on my own or with a partner.

I also have a future goal of improving my public speaking and incorporating singing and dancing into my instruction. When you teach or when you are in front of others, you are presenting. When you are able to speak clearly, you can build a deeper connection with others which is important as an educator.

Parting words:

It's really important to do what you need to do to sustain hope and this includes building a strong network of support. There will be moments of despair but keep moving forward towards the healing and wholeness that is ours and in doing so, you help yourself and become a blessing to others. So even though you've been diagnosed with PNES or whatever condition, you can still make a positive difference in other people's lives, even as you might be struggling in your own. And it will get better, or at least our perspective

of the situation will improve. I wish you love, hope, and healing in your journey of recovery.

BDLR
Isle of Man, UK
March 2015

BDLR is 43 years old and married (second marriage). She has no children. She graduated with a first class honors degree in pharmacy. She was a member of MENSA for several years, joining at 17 years with an IQ of 174. She worked as a pharmacist for a couple years but was forced to stop due to health issues. She holds a Master's degree in Manx Studies (studies of the Isle of Man) and she is a gym instructor by qualification. She is now working from home selling cosmetics and is very happy with this job. She was an UltraRace runner until recently when she was forced to stop running due to some difficulties with her feet. In the past, she has participated in an 11 day race from the north to the south of Ireland and in a walking race around the Isle of Man. In 2008, she completed a 170 mile walk in 47 hours and 22 minutes. She has been featured in the newspapers and on the radio and is a local hero. Over 7 years she ran 7,000 miles and raised £15,000 for charity. In the Olympic games of London 2012, she was honored with carrying one of the 8,000 Olympic torches. She was awarded the torch and it actually now sits in her lounge (her husband brings the torch over so that it can be seen through Skype while the interview is ongoing).

Diagnostic History

I really had two different bouts with NEAD. My first seizure was in 1995, I was 24 years old. By 1998 I did manage to get out of them, stop them with the help of a mental health worker. The second round started in February 2011, a few months before the island run I was going to participate in and I'm still having the seizures even though they are a lot better than they were. We are beginning to get on top of them a bit. My last one was earlier this week. I always think "I'll be okay, I'll be okay" and I wasn't okay. But fortunately, nobody saw me and I was able to look after myself and then I came home after that seizure. I'm having about one a week, at the moment. But I used to have one a day. That was very life-limiting.

How was the diagnosis of PNES/NEAD made in your case, how was it explained to you by that doctor?

To be honest with you, I've never had my diagnosis clearly explained to me. I don't remember actually being given a diagnosis. I've had to put a name to this. Basically, the first lot of seizures in 1995-1998 were called "pseudoseizures" and I was accused of faking it and told that I was a trouble maker. I was on a medical ward for 10 weeks having seizures, they pumped me with diazepam and then they decided it was a psychiatric illness. My first husband, took the fact that I was going to a psychiatric ward really badly, which didn't make things any easier. It was awful, absolutely awful. I had to come back to the Isle of Man with my family in 1997 because I had made many suicide attempts. I was also given other diagnoses: schizophrenia, schizoaffective and borderline disorder. At times I did self-harm. My arms and legs are scarred. I've been to some incredibly bleak places in my time. I went through the psychiatric system on the Isle of Man, from an adult inpatient to a day patient to community living. There was only one staff member, a clinical nurse, who seemed to have any knowledge of how to treat this. He took the time to listen to me and when I was having the seizures I could hear him saying "allow yourself to go into the seizure and really get the seizure out." To be honest with you, it worked and I stopped having seizures in 1998. But, all the other staff in the hospital just really told me off all the time.

Then in 2010 I had a really bad flu and a couple of months after that, my husband and I went to the cinema to see "Black Swan." We didn't realize that the film was actually very "psychological," it was filmed using a hand-held camera for a lot of it. Within 10 minutes of the film starting, I knew I had problems. First thing, I could smell urine and I actually said to my husband "you haven't wet yourself, have you?" Then I started jerking in the seat. I went to the doctor three days later and I had a fit in the waiting room. I was admitted on a ward at the hospital and the very next day I was referred to the Drug and Alcohol team which I declined. Since I have been a psychiatric patient, I have a "P" on my medical notes, I was referred to Drug and Alcohol. I'd only drunk half a pint of cider before that day but I think it was just easier for them to say "oh, she's psychiatric, there must be something related to drugs and alcohol." I couldn't believe it and unfortunately it caused a lot of family problems because there are other family members who have an alcohol problem and my mom thought I was going down the same route. Months later I was able to see a neurologist but when I left the hospital I was still having the same number of fits. Then I saw another neurologist, the EEG was normal with video telemetry, and they concluded "it's not epilepsy," but didn't say anything else. I was referred to see a neuropsychiatrist and he diagnosed me with "conversion disorder." He took his time to explain whatever that was. And then I was referred to a neuropsychologist in 2013 who was actually good. He confirmed the seizures were not epileptic and I should be referred to a clinical psychologist for treatment. I had kept insisting till then that I had epilepsy, not non-epileptic seizures, but at that point I started coming around to accepting that this wasn't epilepsy. I had to wait 5 more months to see the clinical psychotherapist. He saw me for 13 sessions and he went through things like the inner child, various things like that. At the time I didn't think it was helpful. I had three seizures during those thirteen sessions. I found it really difficult. I was angry because it had taken so long to get to this stage and I wondered if I could have done all of this years ago. Fortunately, I have Internet and I have come to understand that what I have is Non-epileptic attack disorder (NEAD) and I have learned more about it.

What do your seizures look like?

I get a feeling I'm going to have a seizure; I have a very intense feeling in my head that I'm going to have a seizure and I need to lie down. I can't think properly. And I certainly can't speak. If I can't find somewhere to lie down, I end up having to say to people "fits, fits" and in fact I have little cards that has "My name is BDLR, I'm going to have a non-epileptic seizure. I need to lie down now". So I lie down, glasses off, hopefully something under my head. It's my upper body that's affected usually. I go very straight for 10, 20 seconds and then sort of shake quite rapidly and I throw my head back. I can hear people saying "oh gosh we don't know what to do." It feels like I am in a different, sort of cloudy place. And then I sort of relax and go totally limp and then it takes me about a minute to be able to start communicating with people. When they ask if I am okay, I can answer "yes". And then gradually, over two/three minutes I am able to sit up and after about twenty minutes, you wouldn't even know I'd had a seizure. I have to sleep. I go to sleep for about an hour. It's not my body that is tired, it's my mind or brain. My husband says these seizures seem to be a way of resetting myself, re-booting.

I find them incredibly embarrassing. If it's just my husband and I, it's fine. But I've had seizures in front of just about everybody I know. I've had that many, and it is embarrassing. I have a medical bracelet on which has come in useful a few times. People know to call my husband, even if it's just for advice. I live in a few small village and we have two chemists in the village. I've actually used both chemists quite a few times when I don't think I can get home quick enough to have the seizure. I really don't like having seizures on pavements because all sorts of things happen like ambulances getting called and people say you are drunk.

Do you know why you have these seizures?

I'm actually becoming more aware of it now. It's stress. I've never been able to cope very well with stress. I may not find something to be too stressful at the time but then later on I will have a fit. The other thing that causes my seizures is a sensory overload: Loud noise, flashing lights, hot, stuffy rooms, any of those can cause me to have a seizure.

The first time I had seizures, I was working in a pharmacy and the job was awfully stressful. At the same time I was married to my first husband who was terribly controlling. I think this contributed greatly to it.

What has your quality of life been like with PNES/NEAD?

It has changed over time. At times, I felt discriminated against for having NEAD. For example, I used to go to a club for adults with mental health problems and when I first started having these seizures back in 2011 I received a letter stating that I was not allowed to attend the club anymore because I was having seizures. My husband and I hit the roof. I needed to do things that were beneficial to help me stop having the seizures and I was being told I couldn't do them. I wondered: what about the asthmatics and diabetics? They're not banned from the club. Eventually they said "you can come back to the club as long as you give a public presentation, you tell everybody what your problem is." So I had to stand in the main room and tell everybody what non-epileptic seizures are and what to do if I had one. So I was forced to tell people I didn't even know some pretty confidential medical information. I've never seen an asthmatic have to give this type of talk... But that did get me back into the club. Now, my quality of life is much better. I am more confident going out since the seizures are happening less frequently.

Do you find that you've experienced any side effects as a result of having these seizures?

My memory's not good at all (e.g. names and faces). It's so embarrassing. And the other thing I have problems with is finding words. I will be speaking and suddenly cannot find the words and I have to try to describe what I'm trying to say. I am especially self-conscious with my mom because with all of the things I've been through and she's had to go through, I don't want her to think I'm drunk or anything.

How has your health been beyond the PNES/NEAD?

I was diagnosed with an under active thyroid three years ago. I also have neuropathic pain in my legs and in my face. I've had this pain only a couple years. I take 15 tablets a day and I'm only 43 years old! I have not been able to do Ultra Runs lately because of the seizures, the tiredness and because I have a bunion. I've got irritable bowel syndrome (IBS) as well which I have had since my early 20's. I have awful problems with my periods as well, extreme pain.

Do you find something helps you cope with your seizures better?

I did a mindfulness course over 8 weeks. Prior to doing it, I used to get quite anxious going to things, especially going to my brass band practice where I play percussion. I would almost have a panic attack, my tummy would hurt and I would have butterflies. But after having done the mindfulness course, I am a lot more relaxed and my seizures have dropped considerably. I took the mindfulness course at a college. It had never been suggested beforehand. When I mentioned it to my psychiatric nurse she said "Oh I think I would be quite good" and so I went. I was a bit skeptical about doing it. I was concerned that I might have a seizure during mindfulness session and I struggled between telling the instructor or not. The problem is that, sometimes, if I go into great detail beforehand about my episodes, they stop me from participating but if I don't tell the person and I have a seizure, I can't explain what's going on before all hell breaks loose. People will say "you should have told us". So I did tell the instructor and she was actually very interested. She had never heard about anything like this and she wanted to know what to do if I had the seizure. We placed a mat at the back of the classroom with a pillow and the idea was if I didn't feel well I would lie down and she would supervise. If she had any concerns she would ring my husband or 999. I briefly told the other participants that I had seizures caused by stress and that I was doing this course to try to get better. As it was, the only seizure I had was in the third class and the teacher was really good. A big fuss was not made and once I felt well enough I got back on the chair and did the rest of the class. What I like about mindfulness is that I could do however much I wanted to do it. Over the 8 weeks we did all sorts of things in that room including mindfulness walking. I have a wooded area down the road and I enjoy walking through that on a nice summer day, to listen to the birds, it's just the most wonderful thing. Now I take time out for myself.

It helps if people are tolerant and understanding. It helps telling people about the seizures because then in my mind I know if I'm going to have a seizure there is a plan in place. I think that probably reduces the stress by actually knowing that others know what to do. It's difficult though because I don't think I'll ever be free of seizures.

I think what has helped me though is to accept that this is not epilepsy, to accept that it's non-epileptic. That has been one of the hardest things to do, it really has. Because I was in denial for so long. I kept insisting: "It's epilepsy, it's epilepsy, I need to go for more and more tests". I have now come to realize that it's okay that it is not actually epilepsy and that knowing this, I can deal with it.

Have you learned anything personally from having PNES/NEAD?

I try not to stress out as much and to talk about things. It's taught me that it should not stop me from doing things and to keep moving forward always.

Do you feel that you have the understanding and the support from your family?

My husband's brilliant [he was in the background during the interview and could be heard saying "thank you"]. Some of my friends are absolutely brilliant as well. However my family has not been as supportive. My family works in the medical field (doctor, pharmacist) so you would think that they would be understanding and we should talk about it in depth, but no. As soon as I mention non-epileptic seizures, there's a silence for a short while and then another conversation comes along and it's really annoying.

What would you like to say to your family about living with PNES/NEAD?

I would just like to have a chat about NEAD, like we chat about other things, just to have a discussion about it, what might be causing it, what might be best, instead of this wall of silence. I can talk to my mom about my nephews until the cows come home but as soon as I mention seizures…

What would you like to tell medical professionals about PNES/NEAD?

I think every case has to be taken on individually and they have to work to understand them. Just because maybe they weren't taught about it in medical school does not mean it does not exist. People living with this condition need a lot of support. Being told that, "oh no it's not a physical illness and we can't give you medication bye, bye" is just not good enough. It would be nice for the Isle of Man to have a support group for people with PNES/NEAD. I talked with my GP and he reckons that there should be 20 people at least with this condition, but where are they?

What are your plans for the future?

It's actually looking really good. I've got two young nephews who are absolutely wonderful, and a lovely husband. I also have a job! I sell cosmetics from my home and on my own schedule. This job has helped me make good friends. I'm actually quite good at doing it.

I also play percussion in a brass band. I've done lots of concerts, carnivals with the band and it's completely changed my life. We play on Monday and Wednesday nights. I did tell them all about non-epileptic seizures and there is a backroom behind percussion where I can go and lie down in if I'm not feeling well. And three members of the band are in the medical field: we have a paramedic, a doctor and a nurse. I also sing in the choir at church. I have been working with the Epilepsy Action. I am the secretary of the epilepsy group I mentioned. They're very keen to have an epilepsy and non-epileptic seizure group. We had our first meeting and I actually talked for a couple minutes to the group about non-epileptic seizures and what the difference is.
I'm the chairman of the Isle of Man Poetry Society so I do poetry. And now that the seizures have gone down in frequency, it's given me a whole lot more self-confidence to go out. I don't take a cushion with me like I used to do to put under my head.

The future is much brighter now. I am so happy with my husband. I'm actually living in <u>our</u> house now (I've lived in 13 different places on the Isle of Man since I came home and at one point was homeless when I first divorced my first husband). Now I have a lovely three bedroom self-detached house with a garden; I've always dreamt of having a lovely garden. I even have my own conservatory here. That's another thing I've always dreamt of having.

GR
New Jersey
March 2015

GR is a 36 year old woman who is married and has 4 children. She is not currently working. She used to work in a storage office for about five years but was also fired five years ago for "insubordination." She had blackouts and the district manager fired her possibly due to some characteristics of the episodes themselves. Ever since then she has had a difficult time with the PNES and has not been able to go back to work.

Diagnostic History

I am not quite sure when the seizures first started, but I sort of assume that it was six, seven years ago. The diagnosis was made through video EEG after I got fired. They said it was abnormal but they didn't know the answer. I was supposed to come back the following month to stay for another video EEG but I never came back. And so what happened was, everything got worse for me. I stayed with the doctors I had, I didn't come back to follow up with the specialist. I was taking medications, on and off but the doctors, nobody was understanding my situation. And then in December 2013, I had the ongoing episodes, so I had to go into the hospital and see the specialist again. So I spent almost a year and a half, two years before seeing him again. My neurologist kind of pushed me away and said that I needed to see the specialist again. So it felt like everybody was sort of pushing me away. So I came back for another video EEG and then I saw the neuropsychologist and everybody and then she explained that I had the PNES seizures.

Do you know why you have these seizures?

I don't really know why I have them. Sometimes I think my emotions could be a trigger. Sometimes I don't know what triggers them because they happen and I don't know why.

How has your experience been working with medical professionals regarding PNES?

There are some big differences in how I have been treated. The old neurologist used to… I felt like he used to push me away all the time, seemed to not be paying me any attention. I tried to explain when everything started but I felt like I wasn't being heard. He used to push me away. When I started to come to the specialist's office, after I saw the neuropsychologist, I felt like I was understood and I was safe. That's how I felt compared to where I was at before because before no one was explaining anything and I felt so lost, not understanding what was wrong with me.
As for other doctors I've had since for other conditions, hey didn't understand either. I bring them the report and everything and nobody ever sticks.

How was your health prior to being diagnosed with PNES?

I had depression and post-traumatic stress. They had diagnosed me with schizophrenia back then, now they changed it to schizoaffective, so I don't know. I was in a psychiatric hospital because I tried to commit suicide and they said I almost had a cardiac arrest. I took a whole bunch of pills and they put me in the hospital. The hospital was helpful and so was the outpatient program but then I had stopped going there because I didn't want to go to the program and that's when everything got all screwed up, the seizures started after all of that.

How would you describe your quality of life?

Well, life for me has been rough; it's always been a struggle. It's hard to deal with and I don't know it's just hard, I don't know how else to explain it.

Do you feel like you have the support of your friends and family with dealing with the PNES?

No I think it's hard. I feel like they don't understand me, so it's hard to get them to understand.

What has helped you the most with the PNES?

I think what's helped me is the change in medication. Seeing the specialist, coming for psychotherapy helped me too. The pain management group that I'm seeing is helping me too.

What would you like to tell others about what it's like to live with PNES and how they can maybe help?

Support, a lot of support would be good. And patience.

What have you learned about living with PNES?

I've learned that I'm not going to die. I've learned that I'm not going to die and I'm not going to go blind. That it's just a sensation, and I learned that my emotions have a lot to do with it, play a big role on the PNES and that's something that I was denying before because I didn't want everybody to think that I am having these just because I'm stressed out. I used to want to take away the stress and not think about that I'm stressed and think about what was going on. On my end, that I was stressed so now I learned that my emotions got to play a big role on the PNES.

Is there something, when you first got the diagnosis that would have helped you?

I wish that when I went through all these problems somebody could have explained it to me way before instead of letting me go from doctor to doctor, from ER to ER. Because I mean, I wanted to know what was wrong but nobody explained it to me so it took a long time. I went through a lot of years dealing with episodes and everything went crazy for me. If they had explained it before, maybe it would have been different. Maybe it wouldn't have been as bad.

*Acceptance is
the
way to
peace.*

The Tao

ME
March 12, 2015
Australia

ME is a 37 year old man who is married and has no children. He and his wife have two dogs. He is a Fitter/Turner (tradesman) and is currently employed at a large hardware company. He is an Australian Army veteran.

Diagnostic History

I had my first seizure in 2008 (7 years ago, more or less). I was in the army out on the range. I was there just in case I could help someone with the weapons being used, but it was actually one of the easiest trips I've done because I'd done all the maintenance and knew nothing was going to break down. It should have been the most relaxing field trip I'd ever done.

The first PNES event started off as a nervous tick in my leg that went on for about an hour. Then that gradually turned into the full grand-mal style seizure (with no loss of consciousness) that I had to endure for the next few years. I was evacuated out but the ambulance broke down within meters of the Aid Post, so we had to search for another vehicle. We were about an hour and a half away from Darwin city. It was a bit of a wild ride with the seizure was still going on continuously throughout the journey. I just wanted it to stop. It didn't matter what it took, I just wanted it to stop. Once we got within mobile phone range, the medics called a civilian ambulance to meet us and then I got loaded up into that and rapidly they put something into me that knocked me out. I didn't regain consciousness until I was in the emergency ward of the hospital. One of the mechanics from my unit stayed with me and then they called my wife in. I stayed at the hospital for a few hours, then was transferred to the military ward on the local barracks.

I was having seizures a couple times a day and they could go anywhere from a couple of minutes to a couple of hours. It hurt, physically and emotionally. After a couple weeks I was given a day with my wife and we went to a massage parlor. I was knotted all over. And when I wasn't having a seizure I was having a hot shower, trying to get the body to stop hurting, or sleeping.

I spent 3 months in a few different military hospitals and underwent all the usual epilepsy tests and cycled through all the usual epilepsy drugs. Eventually, I was flown into Sydney to a specialist down there and it was determined at that time, that what I was having were psychogenic seizures instead of epileptic seizures. Before they actually gave me the diagnosis I had spent a lot of hours online, trying to work it out. It wasn't easy, there wasn't much information but I managed. So I'd actually come to the conclusion before the medical professionals came in to give me the diagnosis. And as soon as the diagnosis was in, it moved on from there. I understand it takes a lot longer for many other people to get their diagnosis but that 3 months was a long time for me. I was having daily seizures, and multiple times every day.

Once I got the diagnosis, the recommendation for treatment was to go see a psychiatrist. But the psychiatrist didn't really know where to go from there. So it was basically me using the psychologist to teach me CBT and working on ways to control the symptoms. Since I was still in the Army at that time I had access to any medical professional I needed.

Do you know why you have these seizures? What has been your understanding of why you have them?

It's a conversion reaction. Basically I had managed to suppress PTSD, anxiety and depression to the point where even I didn't even recognize I had them. It was my subconscious minds way of forcing myself to get the help I needed.

How do you prefer to call your episodes?

I go with PNES. Generally when I talk to medical professionals in Australia they still get referred to as "pseudo seizures." Most of the psychiatrists that I've talked to didn't really know much about PNES but were able to help once they understood it was a conversion reaction aka somatoform disorder.

Are you or have you been in psychological/psychiatric treatment? What is this treatment like? How has it been helpful with the seizures and with other emotional issues? Do you feel you need something more?

Whilst still in the Army I had access to both psychological and psychiatric treatments. Between the two a combination of drug and talk therapy brought the seizures under control. There are underlying issues of PTSD, depression and anxiety. The therapy has helped with the depression and anxiety but more still needs to be done about the PTSD.

How do your seizures look, how do they present themselves to you?

I don't lose consciousness, which is probably a good thing but is hard too, being able to feel your body convulse and not be able to control it is one of the scariest events I have ever endured. I can still speak through the episode. The intense ones look like a grand mal seizure. The smaller ones look like myoclonic jerks, they look similar to the jerky movements of someone with Tourette's. The ones that are the hardest to deal with are pretty much the grand mals. Fortunately, I have never hurt myself other than minor bruising. The actual episodes could last up to an hour, on and off when they were at their worst. Now they're much better controlled (less than once a month) I usually only get small jerky movements for only a few minutes at a time.

Were you ever diagnosed with any other disorder? Any other illness before having been diagnosed with PNES?

I was diagnosed with PTSD a couple of years before the PNES started but very little was done about that. I just suppressed that and then moved on until it hit the trigger point of turning into PNES. I did have the option of seeking treatment of the PTSD in the first case but that would have been very detrimental to my military career at the time. In hind sight I made a very poor choice.

What has been your experience working with the medical professionals?

In my experience most of the medical staff have little understanding of PNES, however they still try to assist. Most of the time their assumption of non-epileptic seizures is that they are caused by drugs, but I can say that I have felt heard and understood by the profession as a whole.

How would you rate and describe your quality of life since developing PNES?

It's changed so much from when the PNES first started to now. When it started, I was still in the Army and never had any intention of getting out. I loved my job, I loved my lifestyle. I had planned to be in the Army until I retired. I had started with the Army Reserve when I was 17 and still finishing high school. I stayed in the Army Reserve for a few years and worked construction job until I deployed to Malaysia and Singapore in a 4 months training exercise, which led me to transferring to the ARA (Australian Regular Army, full time) All up I served for a total of 15 years. Enlisting into the Army was the only job I ever wanted as a kid and I even achieved my dream of being Airborne. Then I moved on to weapons repair (Armourment Fitter). That was my life and my life goals up until everything changed. And all of the sudden it changed. I managed to stay in for three years after the diagnosis.

Now I'm living a much quieter life. It is very different from what I had ever planned but I have truly come to love life. My wife and I have bought a house which is something we never thought we'd do because we kept moving every two years with the Army.

I'm in a job that's much less stressful and I love, so in a way my quality of life has improved.

Have you learned anything from the PNES?

Yes, very much so. It's taught me not to suppress my emotions. It's taught me that it is not a bad thing to actually feel. So it has helped me grow quite a lot. It's been a very hard lesson but one that I am better for learning.

What would you say benefits you the most with coping with your seizures?

By getting that balance right in my life. Having time to go to the gym, to spend time with my wife and my dogs, I love my dogs. By getting that balance back in life between work and free time has helped. Basically keeping overall stress low is the best avoidance of a trigger. If we've coming up to a stressful day at work then I'll be extra careful about what I'm eating, how much sleep I'm getting, that type of stuff. But if there's no extra stress then I can be a little more lenient about scrutinizing food or I can afford to skip a gym session. So it's the overall balance that needs to be protected. My wife and I love going camping too and we've been doing lots of workouts at the pool lately. Apart from that, I'm in a motorcycle club now that the actual seizures are under control. Long rides on the motorbike are a beautiful way to spend a lot of your time.

Do you notice anything that exacerbates your seizures?

Physical illness is a big one. I had pneumonia last year and that threw me off more than I'd like. Apart from that for me ANZAC DAY (Veterans Day) can be a trigger. In Australia it's a really big event. I've found in the last couple of years that it is a trigger and probably always will be. There's a very big media build up to it now. Previously it used to be something that came and went, it was always well respected, but now the media has picked it up a lot more than they used to. So that buildup does create extra anxiety in the lead up to the event.

Have you felt that your family has been supportive and that they understand what this is?

My family's been awesome. I'm really lucky with that. To start with they weren't around much because we were four hours away by the plane, but my family was supportive even when they weren't there physically. It also helped a lot that one of my brothers, was living in Sydney at the time when I was getting treatment down there by the Army, so I got to see him a lot more. When I was getting diagnosed, he was really helpful in finding information and helping me out in that way.

One of the benefits of being out of the Army is that we live near family now, I actually get to see my family a lot, which is awesome. As for friends, I still get to hear from them through Facebook and phone calls. I'm still in touch with one of the medics up there who is now one of my best friends. We often chat a lot. I've joined the Military Brotherhood MMC so I've got a good circle of friends who understand where I've been and help me move forward.

Is there anything you would like to tell health professionals about living with PNES?
One thing is that I've had so many medical professionals tell me how "interesting" this is and I wish they wouldn't. It is many things: painful, terrifying, confusing, but from my point of view

definitely not "interesting." It's probably because it is such an uncommon illness for many medical professionals to encounter. I mean I'm glad that it's rare enough that they don't need to know about it, but please don't tell me it is interesting!

Something that helped me was a book about PNES that came out a couple of years ago. I liked the introduction, just to know that other people had been where I've been and it was nice to know that I wasn't on my own. The only people I have chatted with on Facebook are from Europe or America, not Australia. It made me feel at times like I was the only person in Australia who's been diagnosed with PNES.
I think that once more books gets published on PNES, people will have an opportunity to see and understand more about it. If these books can sit on book store shelves, in doctors' waiting rooms and such, it will assist this information to spread. I think that knowledge is the biggest thing at the moment.

What do you see for your future?

I hope there will come a time where all this is just a memory, something that happened in my past. Until then I try to stay stable, balancing family, work, exercise and fun. I'm not where I need to be in my recovery, but I'm a lot better off that I used to be!

Never give up!

**Kozue
March 2015
Japan**

Kozue was interviewed by her psychiatrist in Japan and this interview was then translated into English. This is the only interview in this book that is written in third person.

Kozue is a 31 year old Japanese woman who is unmarried and has no children. She is college educated. She is currently working at a grocery store; she has been at this position for 8 months. She reports experiences of unemployment due to her PNES in the past. These experiences include when she was 24 years old, she worked at the office of university hospital. But, she had psychogenic episodes often when she left home for the office. As a result, she was frequently late for the work and couldn't get to the office. At that time, she was diagnosed with epilepsy. She had many neurological examinations (without long term EEG) and was treated by many physicians with multiple medications. She was diagnosed with epilepsy mainly because she has a cavernous hemangioma.
But, her psychogenic seizures never stopped despite all the medications. Consequently, she lost her job.

When she was 26 years old, she worked at the private hospital as a social worker, but her psychogenic seizures occurred again. She became disabled and was unable to work because PNES sometimes happened at her work place.

Her seizures began at age 24 years old but she did not receive the proper diagnosis of PNES until she was 26 years old. She was evaluated by a famous epileptologist who told her she didn't have epilepsy and that instead she had PNES. The doctor explained "It just comes from psychiatric problems. It is not uncommon. You will never die from PNES."
She felt that explanation was not enough and she could not accept

this new diagnosis. She felt that that explanation was given in an inattentive and dismissing manner. The doctor gave her the new diagnosis but, he never gave her a new treatment. She felt the doctor did not spend enough time giving her this explanation and she concluded herself that if there is no treatment, she would not accept the new diagnosis. She couldn't accept new diagnosis as PNES because it felt like such a sudden change of diagnosis from epilepsy to PNES and it confused her. It was only when she began the psychiatric treatment with her current doctor that she gradually came to accept the new diagnosis and was able to think of the many stresses and conflicts she had experienced. Now she is able to cope much better with her stress and her feelings.

Do you know why you have these seizures?

She knows that her seizure sometimes happened when she is tired, fatigued or if she has a conflictual interaction with a co-worker or if she has a negative mindset.

She states that she doesn't appreciate the term "psychogenic". Because "psycho" means "mad" or "crazy."

What do your seizures look like? How do you feel after your seizures and what is your recovery time (minutes, hours, days)?

She never loses consciousness. She feels energy in her abdomen and her left arm and leg become rigid. She is unable to control these movements. She used to feel well after having a psychogenic seizure. But, currently she feel only the exhaustion. Her recovery time is half and hour to one full hour.

Are you or have you been in psychological/psychiatric treatment? What is this treatment like? How has it been helpful with the seizures and with other emotional issues? Do you feel you need something more?

She undergoes cognitive behavioral therapy (CBT) training with her doctor who is specialized in psychiatry and epilepsy. Through this treatment she has learned that it is possible to analyze her thoughts and behaviors and to change her thoughts, feelings and behaviors through CBT. Things that have changed include that she used to feel very stressed for a long time before meeting up with her friends. But, now she feel free to meet her friends and is relaxed about this.

She reports that now she feels heard and understood by medical professionals which was not the case before. She has come to see that some of the medical staff are dedicated to working with her and are serious about their commitment.

What benefits you the most when coping with your seizures?

To work with a reliable doctor who is familiar with the treatment of PNES. Now, when PNES is about to happen, she feels she can challenge the seizures and make them stop. She also thinks to herself that if the seizure happens, it is not a big problem. After the seizure stops, it's OK to call the office.

Have you had the support of family and friends?

Yes, she has felt that she has the support of her families and her friends. She is grateful to them.

What would you like to tell others in your life, your family, your friends and your medical professionals, about what it's like to live with PNES and what they can do to help you to heal from this illness?

Don't be excessively afraid. Please know that PNES is not same as other common mental disorders such as depression and anxiety disorder.

She wants her family and friends to know the features of her stress. And she wants to build the better relationship where they can talk each other in a more relaxed manner.
She can't explain this in a few words but now she wants to inform not only the general population but also medical staff about what PNES is. She wants to build a more fluid access to treatment for PNES in Japan and would like to connect with other patients with PNES in Japan and throughout the world.

What do you see in your future?

She will keep working at her current work place. Then she plans to get enough money to prepare for studying in the mental health field. She wants to earn a degree in psychiatric social work. She then wants to participate in patient advocacy.

KMH

March, 2015
Texas

KMH is a 47 year old woman who is married and has 2 biological children and 2 step-children. One of her daughters (aged 24) is disabled (intellectually challenged). She lives with her husband and her 24-year old daughter. She worked as a project manager at the same firm for almost 10 years but was forced to stop working in June of 2014 after developing PNES. She is not currently receiving social security benefits.

Diagnostic history

My first seizure occurred when I was 46. On June 8th I became very ill and I thought that perhaps it had something to do with my thyroid condition. After having my thyroid removed in June 2013, I'd been unstable for some months trying to get the right dosage of thyroid replacement hormones. The preceding Monday I had had to go to the emergency room. I was having quite a bit of chest pain and leg pain that they thought it might have been a blood clot. We went through a series of tests and 2 additional trips to the emergency room; the entire week was quite unsettling. While I was having a sonogram done on the area where my thyroid used to be, I had my first seizure. The lab technician didn't know what was going on and I ended up in the emergency room. After an MRI and a CT scan came back normal it was determined by the ER doctor that it was PNES. He sent me to a neurologist who conducted a 1 hour EEG and he also determined it was PNES. I saw another neurologist who did a 3-day EEG and also determined it was PNES. I never went back to my work place because I became so ill. I lost about 24 pounds in about 4 weeks and at one point my general practitioner wanted to put me in the hospital on a feeding tube for a while because I was so sick. I had lost so much weight that my head would shake all the time. I literally didn't have the strength to keep it up and I couldn't walk unassisted. Even when I wasn't having a full-blown seizure, I shook.

What do your psychogenic seizures look like?

I do not lose consciousness or become paralyzed but I do sometimes lose control over my legs and arms and am not able to talk or walk. Other times only my right arm moves uncontrollably and I can talk but it is very hard and takes a bit to get the words out. I'd say they look a lot like an epileptic seizure. Sometimes the seizures make me very ill and I'm sick with them for days at a time. Other times I recover from them very quickly and am able to get right back to what I was doing before it started.

Do you know why you have these psychogenic seizures?

I've been told it's due to my body's inability to handle stress and anxiety and this explanation makes sense. I guess I am the average married too young, babies too soon, controlling first husband and difficult divorce woman that happens all too often but nothing that I thought would ever lead to this illness. My therapist assures me all the trauma (47 years worth) lives in a place deep down in my brain that I'm not aware of. My step-son just spent 4 years in prison. Raising him was very difficult. My step-daughter is also a recovering drug addict. My son never forgave me for getting a divorce from his dad. Second marriages are always hard. None of this happened overnight. There was a lot of chronic stress. I also had lots of trauma as a child, I was sexually abused and there was substance abuse: your typical dysfunctional family. No one is immune from some difficulties growing up.

I also have hypothyroidism; before that I had Hashimoto's thyroiditis which led to my thyroid being removed in 2013. I will always believe that the surgery and subsequent thyroid issues after the surgery had something to do with me developing PNES. After I had my thyroid taken out, I became hypothyroid, so I gained about 45 pounds but after the seizures, I lost so much weight and I have only regained 8 lbs. since then. So I just keep different sizes of clothes in my closet (laugh). I hate anything thyroid related, since I don't have one anymore. I have this tiny pill I take every day to keep things stable in my body. I only recently found an endocrinologist in Dallas who was able to confirm what I knew all along and she's been very helpful. I think we're on the verge of getting a thyroid medication fixed.

What helps you cope with your PNES?

Knowing that once one starts it will end, my therapy, keeping very busy, my faith, my family and friends support and journaling.

What contributes to your episodes?

Loud noises, strobe lights in movies, lots of people being around, stress, lack of sleep, way too much stimulation, fear of new situations.

Have you experienced any changes since developing PNES?

It's changed my/our lives forever. So much is so different now. I don't work. I can't drive for long stretches of time. I have to rely on others for transportation for myself and to take my daughter to work during the day because my husband is at work. My parents sold their house where they'd lived for 17 years to move by me and my family. Their dog was so traumatized by the move that they had to take him out of state to live with my sister. I feel like I'm keeping my husband and myself from our retirement dream of owning a small farm. I worry a lot about my daughter who is disabled. Who will take care of her if I get worse? I now fear new situations and only keep to familiar places and people.

At first, it never really entered my mind that I wouldn't go back to work. But the Friday before I was supposed to go back to work on a part-time basis, I got a call from our HR lady. She said "You can't come back to work on Monday because you have a disability and we have to make sure our office is set up to handle someone with your disability. Now my doctor's letter clearly said that I was not disabled any more than someone with epilepsy or diabetes or anything. I explained that I have generalized anxiety and that no accommodations needed to be made for me. I explained that if I did have a seizure I would appreciate it very much if someone did come to my office and make sure I didn't fall out of my chair, or hold my hand or whatever, some sort of comfort, but that I have never hurt myself or anything else in the process. So a week went by and I had really prayed about it and I realized it was an extremely stressful job that required 60/65 hours a week. I was never off the clock. And so I called the owner of the company and told them that I could only work 20 hours a week (instead of the 32 they were requesting) and that they probably needed to find someone to fill my position. And I never went back. And I was extremely relieved after that. I had the longest stretch of seizure free days that I've ever had-22 days. I directly attribute those 22 days to having left that job. And in the interim I started to work at a customer service job. But apparently I don't like being yelled at by mad customers all day and I had a seizure when I was on the phone with a customer on what would have been my 23rd day. I should have thought right then and there that that was a little bit too much stress a little too soon. And that company was very understanding but I don't want to go back there.

Are you in psychological/psychiatric treatment?

I am currently in therapy with a VERY nice lady doing CBT, EFT (tapping) and neuro-feedback. I feel that it has helped tremendously. She is a psychologist and she specializes in PTSD, stress and anxiety disorders among other things. We do neuro-feedback twice a week and then cognitive behavioral therapy and EFT once a week. After my first appointment with her I went 29 days without a seizure; the longest stretch by a week that I'd had since June. Before that it was only 8 days. At this time I feel like my sessions with my therapist are all that I need.

I have been seeing her about 6 weeks now. It took me a long time to find her. At first I was in therapy for a little over 3 months, but that therapist moved me to a bench when I had a seizure and left me out there alone. She didn't bother to get anyone. I stopped treatment with her because of that. And then I went into denial and wouldn't talk about my diagnosis and didn't want any help from anyone. I just wanted to ignore it. It would go away. I was just going to wish it would go away. And then I had a situation in January and realized "Okay, I need some help" so we found my current therapist and I've been working with her ever since.

I also see my psychiatrist for medication. He treats me more for the anxiety and depression side of things and we leave the PNES stuff up to my psychologist.

How would you describe your family and friends reaction to your PNES? Have you felt supported?

Totally!! My parents sold their house and moved closer to where we live. My husband has been incredibly supportive too. I couldn't ask for anything more from my family or friends; they are all so supportive and have been here for me 100%. I live with my daughter who is intellectually challenged but very high performing and she's the best too. She is on the ball about my meds. She says things like: "maybe you shouldn't be eating that" and "did you get enough sleep?" My mom and I are members of one of the Facebook PNES groups and it really breaks my heart how many people go through this alone.

As for out of the home, I've only had one seizure out of my home, in the lobby of where we get our hair cut and the people were very understanding and helpful.

We have all educated ourselves about PNES too. I found a book on PNES and I read it immediately after the diagnosis. Then my husband read it and my mom read it and my dad read it and I currently have it on loan through the Kindle app. My psychologist is now reading it.

What have you learned, personally, from having PNES?

Don't over-think things. Stress less. Relax more. I've learned to ask for help when I need it and to accept it when it's offered. I have come to realize "this is my new normal." This is my new life. We're going adjust to it and we're going be fabulous. "And I'm gonna be the best shaker in the county and there you go" (laugh).

I have also learned to journal everything. Even what I eat, when I eat it and what type of supplements and vitamins I take and that sort of thing. Those journals have really come in handy as I moved from one neurologist to another because there were times over the summer where I literally couldn't remember. But because I would write everyday, I can go back and read it.

Reading the book I found on PNES gave me so much hope also because my greatest fear was "what if I'm stuck like this?" The main thing is to not lose hope and to continue, continue forward.

Even my friends and family have learned to limit their stress and they're really trying to relax more. We spend a great deal more time together as a family and enjoy each other more and our time more.

What has been your experience in working with medical professionals? Have you felt heard, understood or validated by the medical profession as a whole?

Everyone that I've worked with has been really great. I did though have a therapist that had no idea what she was doing and that prolonged my finding really good help by a long time. My psychiatrist I've known for years and I get the feeling that if we didn't go back more than 10 years that he'd probably have asked me to find another one. He doesn't believe in PNES and will not use the word PNES. He calls them pseudo-seizures. He won't acknowledge PNES although he's seen me have several episodes. He just doesn't. The neurologists are quick to shovel you from one to another. My primary care physician actually told me to "stop having those silly fits" and my short term/long term disability provider told me that they didn't have a code for my illness in their system therefore I must not have a real illness. I was only awarded 3 weeks disability even though I haven't worked since June 2014. And one therapist that I was seeing for group and individual counseling had me moved onto a bench in the hall of her office building when I was having a seizure during a group session.

What would you like to tell others in your life, your family, your friends and your medical professionals, about what it's like to live with PNES and what they can do to help you to heal from this illness?

I'd like to tell the medical professionals that this illness is REAL and that we deserve the same respect as anyone else with an illness. It's like living in a box and sometimes you can get out and sometimes you cannot. It's like you're trapped in your own mind at times. Triggers that you didn't know you have, present themselves at the most inopportune times.

I wish I knew more people locally like myself so that I could start a local support group where we could actually meet in person and share together. I don't want anyone to be alone and I can try and offer as much support as I can. To know that I have so much support and that there are so many people that don't and their medical professionals won't listen to them and it takes them so long get diagnosed. I am so lucky, I mean I was diagnosed in the emergency room.

You have to learn to live life because you see what can happen to you if that little place in your head can't take it anymore and Pandora's Box opens. There you go and your life is changed forever and your family's life is changed forever. Those of us who have PNES, we're not different from others. No one with this diagnosis is any different than anyone else. Our brains just click a little differently, and that's all. We just want to be understood, to know that we are not alone. Perhaps I have a different perspective because my daughter is disabled and for 24 years we've had people treating her differently and we have had to work to get her the respect that she deserves, that we all deserve. People living with PNES deserve that too.

What do you see in your future?

I am currently looking for employment and I had to file to collect unemployment. I can collect unemployment for up to 26 weeks. It's nowhere near what you would have made in a workplace but it's enough to cover my health insurance and my therapy. And of course as part of that, you are required to look for a job. So I have been actively seeking unemployment and I've had a couple of interviews. I'm very upfront with potential employers even though I don't have to be by law. As someone who used to hire people and had people work for me, I prefer disclosure and that up-frontness. I believe that in two of the positions that's exactly why I didn't get the job. And that's fine, it wasn't meant to be. I don't want to work at a place that isn't going to work with me.

GC
South Africa
April 29, 2015

GC is a 33 year old woman who is married and has no children. She does have two dogs. Her highest level of education is a Masters in Psychology. She has a second degree in the financial field where her highest level is an honors in accounting. Until the end of March of this year, she was employed at the university where she had quite a senior position as a deputy director in the Finance division and was responsible for a very large account. Now she has shifted her career goals and will be working as an Executive Business Coach. She has chosen this career because it combines her two fields of interest.

Diagnostic history

My seizures started in 2007 so I was about 25 years old. It took about three months before I was diagnosed. At first I was diagnosed with epilepsy and they gave me medication and then once they saw that didn't help the neurologist referred me to another neurologist who had video EEG equipment. After I had been there for 48 hours, he came and he told me "what you're having is not epilepsy, it is conversion disorder. There is a conflict in the unconscious that is manifesting as a seizure." I felt that the way he explained it was very sensitive. He certainly wasn't telling me "you're faking it" but still it left me confused. Epilepsy is a disorder that is well known but conversion disorder or PNES are not. I did not know anyone who had been diagnosed with PNES before. There was limited information about PNES available in South Africa. He went on to suggest therapy and asked if there's a therapist that I'm already using because otherwise he could recommend me to someone. At first I didn't accept his recommendation because I was working with someone already. But I found after a few sessions with that psychologist that he didn't really understand non-epileptic seizures and we weren't going anywhere. He seemed focused on stress and wanted to do a coping/stress quick fix for me so after a few sessions I phoned the neurologist. The psychologist that he referred me to was 50 minutes away and as I was not allowed to drive a car my mother had to take me. We decided we had to make the effort and I started seeing her twice a week. It was not an easy process but therapy was the right treatment. The therapist used a combined approach that was mostly psychodynamic. She definitely did make the difference because she knew PNES and had treated it before.

A year after I was diagnosed, I was told by the neurologist that since I was "completely free of non-epileptic seizures" I could start driving. My last seizure was at the end of October 2007. I think this was possible because I got the right diagnosis quickly and went to the correct psychologist. My psychologist helped me with the process of exploring things and realizing "I'm living someone else's life" and helping me make changes. I realized that I was trying to please others and would do anything to avoid conflict. Once I started taking some psychology classes which was my passion, the seizures started decreasing. The more I moved in the direction of doing things I really enjoyed, the seizures became less and less.

What would your explanation be of why you have these seizures?

From a very young age I was always the best at everything I did. I played professional hockey, was at the top of my class in academics and held many leadership positions. I was a very high achiever and when it came to "what I wanted to do?" I didn't actually know what I wanted to do because everything that I did I was good at. My parents are teachers and in South Africa you don't really earn that much as a teacher so I felt I was a child with the brains and had to earn a lot of money, be a successful businesswoman. So family dynamics were at play and I felt there was pressure on me. A part of the therapy was getting my parents in to discuss this (they came in for a couple of sessions). We had to do a lot of inner work until I could really feel that they were sincere in saying "you can be what you want."

What did your seizures look like?

In the beginning it was only my legs that would shake and then later on it became full body shaking, on the ground, and I could hear the people speaking around me so I was aware that there were others. The duration also increased. It might have started as just a few minutes and later on it was more like twenty minutes long and they could happen up to 8 times a day. I could feel it coming on, I would sometimes get a sense and I would try to get myself into a room or a safe place. They could happen anywhere which meant at the end of the day even though I liked running, I wouldn't go even for a walk because I was too afraid to get seizures in the neighbor's lawn or something like that. So my quality of life changed completely from being a very outdoors and social person to just being alone and not wanting to speak to people or have people visiting me. I had to leave my job. They put me on sick leave. I had to stop driving and had to move back to my parents' house. I really became like a baby, back to that phase where your parents are picking up after you. Maybe I wanted to relive those times... And then my therapist suggested doing creative things and I started doing art classes and I really enjoyed that. Even though I would sometimes have a seizure in the art class it was fine for me, it was a safe place for me and I felt I could express myself there and I was amazed at the stuff I could create. I also started doing some yoga, just some stretches. I didn't go to group classes at that stage but later on when I got rid of the seizures and they became way less I started doing yoga and I definitely enjoyed that. Yoga was something my therapist suggested to improve my ability to calm my mind and relaxing my body.

My therapist also recommended that I move out of my parents' house even though I have having seizures, but less than before. It was good for me to be my own person and part of that is living on your own. So I moved to a flat close to the University so I could walk everywhere. There were times when I had seizures but it was way less and it was actually fine and I was able to do my own things again.

What have you learned from having PNES?

I always knew that working in the financial field was not my passion but the problem is that it's always easy to get work in that field. The salary that I was earning was great but I was not happy at work. I could actually feel my body telling me "listen, you're again not doing what you want to do". I realized that I was falling back into my old way and living the life that I thought was expected of me. Luckily, one of the lessons I learned from having PNES was that just because you are good in your work does not mean that you have to do it. There are other jobs and opportunities out there may be a better fit for me. It is important to listen and trust your inner-voice. Therefore, I decided to listen to my body and resign. Taking the step was a leap of faith. Looking back now I knew I made the right decision as it opened up new opportunities. I don't think that I would have made a difficult decision as that if it was not for the lessons I learned from having PNES.

I believe in the mind-body connection and that you have to listen to your body. The body gives us signals and we need to learn to listen to it. I'm definitely more in-tune with my body after having PNES. It is important for me to learn from past experiences. Otherwise history is just going to repeat itself. That is something that I really don't want. I do believe that we always have something to learn from our experiences and that life is a learning curve.

Were you healthy before you started having PNES?

I was a very healthy person physically when the seizures started. But when I first moved to university and started studying accounting I became very depressed. I think that was the real beginning. I was institutionalized and I received electro-therapy. After that I felt fine and asked myself "am I going to continue doing my accounting?" and I decided yes. This was before the seizures started. I took some anti-depressants for two years or so and then I was completely fine. If I had listened then could that have changed things? But I did not develop the skill to really understand myself and have a critical mind, to stand up for what I wanted and that's when my body started telling me "listen!"

My brother has epilepsy and so does my mother's brother. So epilepsy runs in the family. It's like your body unconsciously knows what is getting attention.

Do you find that anything helped you in particular when you were having seizures to deal better with them?

Stretching helped. I also liked to put some classical music on and I had a teddy bear. My brother was in London and he came to visit us and he brought me a teddy bear. It was one of those that you press and it will speak. You can do a live voice recording. And the voice recording said "GC, I love you" or something like that. I would press it all the time and just cuddle the teddy bear. I also wrote a lot of poetry, drawing and painting. The breathing exercises were also very calming.

I think my coping style was avoidant before. I realized I needed to be able to face this stuff and move through it. Now, I can deal with stress without having a seizure and really seeing that I can do it and believing in my own capabilities is a huge thing. Life is stressful. You can't avoid stress. It is important after you've been diagnosed to not avoid stressful situations the whole time. You have to put yourself in stressful situations again because that's the only way you'll see whether you've improved your ability to cope with stress.

Was there anything would exacerbate the seizures?

Stress, not getting enough sleep and conflict. There was a big fight once with my brother and my parents and I had a very big seizure. I was always that child who would be the one to will make peace with everyone. My sister would act out or my brother would act out and I would be the one that tries to solve the conflict. Another thing that seemed to trigger me was sugar and caffeine. So I changed my diet. I tried to not drink any caffeine at that time and not as much sugar.

Do you feel you've had the understanding of your family, friends and others?

Yes, yes, yes. They are wonderful parents, they are always looking out for us. They were very loving and caring. Just after the diagnosis, when we all had to figure out how to deal with the disorder, their love and intense care felt a bit suffocating for me. I was able to forgive them because I realized that 'there is an expiration date on blaming your parents' and that they did what they thought was the best for me at that stage. They were also willing to go for the therapy and to work on themselves. That's been amazing. We have a way better relationship now. My whole family does. Because they were willing to go through the rough stretch with me and didn't resist the work; that was amazing.

As for my friends, there was definitely a shift happening with them. Some of them have come to visit me and have been there with me but it was a bit difficult for them. They didn't really understand this new person that I had become. So there are definitely people now that aren't friends with me anymore. I feel that I could have less friends now because you choose your friends and then you stick with the ones you know understand you and appreciate the deeper side of life. I like friends that can have various perspectives on life. Some of the ones I lost were very religious, I grew up in a very traditional Christian home and some of them thought my seizures were "from the devil" so that was not very helpful... So those friends moved away. There are some that stayed but there's actually very few people that really stayed. It was really a very small group of people that stayed. The few that remained my friends will be friends for life.

As for my husband, he met me when I started with psychology and I had to earn some money to support my studies so I started to work in his company in the finance field. I wasn't having seizures anymore then. So, he never saw that side of me. Even though I don't get seizures anymore I'm sometimes afraid that they are going to come back. He once went with me to the psychologist to understand how to act towards me when I'm afraid that the seizures might start. Sometimes if I have a bad day I overreact and he's very supportive. When I did my research on PNES for school, he was very supportive. He is not just my husband but also my best friend and someone that makes me believe that I can achieve the things I want out of life.

What would you like to tell your friends about what it's like to live with PNES or what would you like to tell your family?

I think one of the things is that I would like them to know just how very difficult it was for me and to acknowledge that it was a traumatic time in my life when I had PNES. In a way I had PTSD after that for a while. It's always going to be a chapter in my life, but I don't want that chapter to become the book. It's a part of me, but it does not define me. It was a very lonely route. It takes your dignity. Rebuilding your confidence and going out in the world again, often having all of these seizures, was hard. I think that was a time in my life when I felt lost and so alone in this world and you can't really explain it to someone that wasn't there. It was a traumatic and lonely experience but I'm grateful for the things I've learned.

What would you tell someone who's been just diagnosed with PNES?

When I meet people who have just been diagnosed with PNES, I tell them "this is amazing because you're on the right track. This is the beginning of the healing process." In a way it's a celebration of sorts because you've got the right diagnosis. Then the most important thing is to find the right therapist and don't settle for one if you feel you're not happy or you're not connecting with that person. Be kind towards yourself and care for yourself. It is not selfish, it is self-care. I find that people with PNES are too often there for others and are afraid to do some self-care. This is your time to really look at yourself and by working on yourself, you will be able to make others happier again. You should really use this time as a gift to be with yourself.

It's important that people realize that they can have an amazing life after being diagnosed with PNES and that they are still capable individuals. If you'd told me eight years ago (when I had PNES) that my life would turn out the way it did, I would not believe you. Wonderful things can happen when you start being true to who you are. One day I will hopefully be a successful business women and I would then like to say "listen I've had non-epileptic seizures but it did not stop me from achieving my goals." Because sometimes you need examples of people that have made in the world out there and that have overcome PNES. I believe that if you can overcome PNES you can overcome any obstacle that life put in your way.

What do you see in your future?

In the future I would like to do my PhD. There was a time when I thought that I wanted to do my PhD on PNES. At the end I decided not to pursue my PhD in this field because I felt it was too close to me. When I was diagnosed with PNES I decided that I wanted to do research in the field to create more awareness. I really enjoyed the research in the non-epileptic field and I think it was part of my healing process as well. I ran a support group for a while and the members would often ask me to tell them about my non-epileptic seizures. I found that it left me stuck in the past. I realized that I did what was necessary to start research in the field in South Africa and that others (such as my supervisor) can take it further. I wanted to plant the seed. I learned that's what I'm good at. I'm good at identifying gaps, planting seeds and initiating the growing process but I don't need to be there for the full growing period. So I'm letting go of it. I have come to accept that just because I had PNES, I don't need to make it my life's calling. I recognize that the research process made it clear to me that I'm very interested in the mind-body connection field.

In the nearer future I want to work in the mind-body connection space. That is why I am pursuing a career as an integral coach (that focuses on mind-body connection) in the business environment. I am passionate about people and want to assist others in developing their potential. It's important for me to enjoy my work and to feel that I'm adding value. Apart from coaching I would like to would like to do more facilitation and consultation. I'm currently changing careers, which is challenging in many ways.

You have to believe that you are good enough and work hard at what you want. So for me it's about really trying, the whole time being true to myself. That's my mission to be as true to myself as possible.

*In the end,
only three things
matter:
how much you loved,
how gently you
lived,
and how gracefully you let
go of things
not meant for
you.*

Buddha

JM
Minnesota
April 2015

JM is a 35 year old woman, who is not married and has no children (she mentions jokingly that she did have a service dog who is in heaven now and if that might count as a child). She is a High school graduate. She explains that she is in a day program for people with traumatic brain injuries and she is on the work crew there shredding paper, putting nails into jars or into boxes and sometimes she volunteers at the Ronald McDonald House cleaning the community room. She receives disability benefits because of blindness and cerebral palsy (CP). She has been completely blind since 2001. She has been in 2 group homes since she has been 29 years old and moved into the 2nd group home about 2 years.

Diagnostic History
I don't really know at what age I started having seizures. I was finally tested at age 16 and they said that I had both epileptic and non-epileptic seizures. And when I was 21 I believe, I did in-patient EEG and that was not a very good experience because of the doctor. When they discharged me, they said that I was having epileptic seizures and that I needed to be on medication, but when we got the discharge papers it said that I was not having epileptic seizures and that I had non-epileptic seizures… So when we called the doctor to talk to him about it he refused to talk to us and had his nurse tell us, not to call anymore. So I still don't technically know if I have the correct diagnosis. When I went for a second opinion, I was hospitalized for 10 days and didn't have a

single episode, but the doctor concluded that I was having non-epileptic seizures, but it wasn't confirmed really.

What do your seizures look like?

I recently had a seizure at my physical therapy appointment and this is how it was described: My left arm flexes up and then I have shaking on the left side of my body, my arm and my leg and then after the seizure itself I'm really lethargic and all I want to do is sleep and my balance is really bad for about a day. Before the seizure itself I know something is going to happen because the right side of my head hurts and then eventually I'll get a weird feeling on the left side of my tummy. During the seizure itself, I can't communicate or hear. I also lose urine during the seizure. I don't quite know how long they last. My group home has a protocol for my seizures; they check on me 15 minutes after they start, so since they don't actually stay with me for the seizure itself, I don't know. I'm trying to get my protocol changed but my group home agency doesn't want to make the change.

My seizures have changed over time but I don't know what they were like before so I can't be specific. It's just what I have been told. I am also off all seizure medications now, but since they took me off of them, my seizures are more frequent and intense.

Do you know why you have these seizures?

I do not because I have not had anything traumatic happen in my life so I really do not have any idea. I wish I knew, it might make things a little easier.

Were you ever diagnosed with any other disorder? Any other illness before having been diagnosed with PNES?

I was born twelve weeks early. I was one pound, thirteen ounces and was exactly 12 inches long. I was in the NICU two months, two weeks and two days. I was about 20 years old when I was diagnosed with cerebral palsy (CP). I kept having muscle spasms in my legs growing up and finally I got tired of this and pursued a diagnosis and they came back with CP. Before that I did I did everything I possibly could and when I was in middle school and high school. I did track and field for the blind school. I got medals every year. In school, I did the best I could. I got mostly B's and C's, but that didn't stop me from trying.

I moved to a group home in 2009 because I got a blood clot in my left leg in 2006 and because of that and the CP I literally couldn't walk and I had to learn how to walk all over again and I was in a nursing home for about 3 years.

How do you prefer to have your condition called?

I have heard everything under the sun, the only one I have not been personally called is Nonepileptic attack disorder which is the one in the UK. I prefer to call them "seizures" because really that's what they are. And right now they call them "events" at my group home but my mom and I call them ""seizures." I am beginning to really hate the word "events." I definitely do not think they should be called "episodes" or "attacks." I always love it when that debate comes up on-line about how this should be called because it always sparks a lively conversation.

Have you noticed anything exacerbates your seizures?

The one thing I have noticed that seems to trigger me is being tired or when I do not get enough sleep.

What's been your experience working with medical professionals?

Since I don't get the ambulance called on me I don't have too much experience with EMT's but my physical therapist that I just had is also an EMT and she said to me no matter what it's called, it's still a seizure and you still have to stay with the person and you still have to show respect. As for nurses, I've been told by some nurses that "we don't have to stay with you during the seizure because it's not hurting your brain so we don't have to take it seriously". I've been told by other doctors and other healthcare people "oh you're just faking it to get attention."
As for my psychiatrist, he feels that these are definitely seizures. It doesn't matter what type they are, they all should be taken seriously. He wants to send me back to neurology right now but I'm not so sure I want to go back to neurology because of the experience I had before.

The psychologist I see is really good. She talks with me about anything stressful that goes on before I have a seizure, we talk about how I feel and then we also talk about if there's any issues in my life that are particularly stressful. We work on different coping methods and she gives me "homework." She had me find an app with relaxing sounds like waterfall or the ocean waves. Sometimes

I do the frogs, and it just gives me something else to listen to and then I can sit and think about my service dog and maybe read or something at the same time. It has helped me cope better with stress. We're also working on communicating with others before I snap. So, for example, if I am feeling upset I tell the group home staff "hey I'm going into shutdown mode right now." I see her once every two weeks. I think I have seen her for about three or four years.

Do you feel that the seizures have affected your quality of life and if so, how?

They have affected my quality of life because if there's an outing planned at my group home, if I have a headache, they won't take me on that outing because they think something is brewing. And when I do have a seizure, because my staff has been told that they don't have to take it seriously, they treat me way different than my housemate who actually has epilepsy. And I don't think it should be like that. So I don't even like to talk about the seizure issue because it is such a touchy subject with me and I tend to go into meltdown mode or get very sad. I have fallen; I've hit my head and I've had multiple concussions throughout my life so far but even with that, they maintain their protocol.

Has your family been supportive throughout all of your diagnosis and with your PNES?

My mom is the most supportive. My dad supports me in ways that are possible for him. Right now my mom is frustrated with the lack of respect I'm getting from my house staff when I have a seizure. But she doesn't know what to say to me and they have been living out of state for about 5 years.

I call my mom every single day and they come back up to Minnesota about once or twice a year and then I go down to where they live once a year for a week. My brothers live out of state too. I have a lot of friends here at my day program and I have a friend that I call every single day. And I'm always looking for people to add to it. Within the last two months I found the Non-epileptic seizures support group on Facebook. That helped me a lot because I can go on there and say "hey this is how my staff treat me" and people understand and they can write back helpful things. That has helped a lot because I actually have people I can talk to who understand exactly what I'm going through. It's an awesome group.

Is there anything you would tell your family about these seizures and anything you want to tell them about what you feel that it's like living with PNES?

I don't have anything really to tell my family but I do have things that need to be said to my group home staff. I would tell them like "hey, I'm not doing this to get attention, I'm not purposefully doing it and I would want you to know how bad it makes me feel when people act like I am purposefully doing it and they feel they don't have to take it seriously.

I would also like to tell that doctor who told us to never call back to his office, that he never should have become a neurologist in the first place. I would encourage him to get his facts straight before he treats patients like that and to be more respectful and to have a better bedside manner.

As for my friends, I just wish I could tell them thank you for being my friend and thank you for understanding that these seizures do happen and for recognizing that I don't do it for attention.

What do you see in your future?

I don't know what I see in my future but I hope someday that there will be an acceptance throughout the medical professional of these as real events and real issues. I hope that in the future, we will no longer be made to feel like we're "psycho patients" and that we are treated in a civilized manner.

AC
Texas
April 2015

AC is 26 years old. She is single and has no children. She is in a relationship. She has a Bachelor's degree with a double major in Sociology and Psychology. She currently works as a substitute teacher and is working towards becoming a full time teacher in the fall.

Diagnostic History:
My seizures started at 19. I started having unexplained seizures so they took me to the hospital, ran tons of tests and we knew that right away that it wasn't epilepsy. The doctors said it was possibly stress induced, possibly doing too much at school, they weren't really sure and released me. To my recollection, they did not recommend I see a psychologist or a psychiatrist. I saw a good amount of neurologists after that, probably about 6 over the years and none of them really understood or helped. I was turned away several times because they said they couldn't see me because they really didn't know what was going on: "If it's not epilepsy there's nothing we can do so we won't give you an appointment". So the way we kind of came to learn about PNES was through my mom who kept researching it for many years, she called around the country trying to find answers, anything that would help. And then we came across a book on psychogenic non-epileptic seizures and when we read it, it really hit home. It helped us come to terms with what I have and how to deal with it. It helped me know what kind of treatment to look for too.

What do your seizures look like?
They vary, for about the 6 years the seizures looked the same. I would make noises and then my whole body would convulse pretty rapidly and they would last an average of 8 minutes. As I started getting better at recognizing when they were coming, they changed. Kind of like "hey you're dealing with it but we need to get this out in a different way." I see it like my body fought back. I started having slurred speech, rapid eye movement, I became paralyzed, couldn't speak, had a lot of confusion, dizziness, things of that nature and that lasted for several hours. And now it's evolved again, kind of back to the original convulsing but they're much less severe and they don't happen as often. My most recent seizure was last night.

Before, when the seizures were over, I used to feel really exhausted and had pain all over my body to the point that if a sheet touched me it would hurt. When I started wanting to work full time I started training myself to get up right away, which isn't to say I can do that every single time but the more I do that, the more my body goes "okay you don't have to lay here in pain." The pain continues. It's just I try to put it in the back of my mind and keep going because I have such a determination to not let this win. I may fall ten times trying to stand up after a seizure but I see that as ten times more motivation to get up.

Do you know why you have these seizures?

I think I have them because I've been through quite a bit. When I was 3 my father started molesting me; that lasted until about 8 years old. That sort of started the cycle of not recognizing healthy boundaries, of being in bad relationships, which led to a very abusive relationship when I was 17. That boyfriend sexually assaulted me on many occasions and I had no idea that it was wrong. And then unfortunately after I started having the seizures I felt so damaged that I continued the cycle of unhealthy relationships. I felt as though no one would want to be with me or love me because I was "damaged" from the abuse and from the fact that I had seizures. Then, I was sexually assaulted by someone who was supposed to be a friend. Therefore, I have a lot of triggers that remind me of these traumatic events. If I am triggered, I am way more likely to have a seizure - especially before I started Cognitive Behavioral Therapy (CBT).

Are you in treatment for PNES now? What is that like?

I now see a psychologist who is trained in CBT which was the recommendation that my mom and I read about in the PNES book we found. She is awesome and really works with me on healthy relationships, changing those thought patterns of being damaged and it's been great. I've been with her for about 6 months. My psychologist didn't know about PNES so she read the PNES book I had found and she went on to read some outside resources. I think she's been able to help a lot because she was willing to go the extra mile.

I also see a psychiatrist for generalized anxiety and I am taking medication for that. It took me a while to find this psychiatrist because before that I bounced through several who didn't understand PNES. Although this one doesn't totally get it, he's willing to listen which is so key. Other psychiatrists just told me repeatedly to "see a neurologist."

What would you say has been your experience working with medical professionals?

ER physicians and nurses for the most part tended to not believe me or thought I took drugs or something of that nature. I even overheard a nurse one time say "she's faking it" and I thought to myself "if I were going to fake something, it's wouldn't be a seizure". Neurologists brushed me aside "we don't know what it is, see someone else." They never provided us with a referral or more information so it was left to my mom and me to do our own research.

There was one positive experience. Not too long ago, I went to the ER and there was a doctor who had trained in Scotland. He was extremely understanding and patient and kind and put me at ease that not everyone was thinking that I was making it up.

Have you noticed any changes, side effects after having started to have these seizures?

I have noticed a change in my memory. I actually got my memory tested when I first started seeing the psychologist 6 months ago and my memory is so bad they had to re-test me several times. And my anxiety has increased a lot! I also have trouble with balance and frequent headaches.

How would you describe your quality of life since you developed PNES?

It was definitely worse at the beginning and it's gotten a lot better over the past year or so. Before having PNES, I used to describe myself as vibrant. I'm just now starting to describe myself that way again. When the seizures first started it was very scary. Everywhere I went I would look for an exit plan if I had a seizure. I hid a lot in bathrooms. Over time, I learned to tell when the seizures were coming. I had a small window of opportunity to get somewhere I considered safe, which was often in a bathroom because I could hide. As much as possible, I tried to hide the seizures from others, even those close to me. I was incredibly embarrassed and ashamed. I felt as though I should be able to control the seizures and stop them and I couldn't. I felt like a burden to everyone around me. I'm slowly beginning to not be ashamed and to be proud of how far I've come. I'm learning to place the blame on the perpetrators rather than myself.

Would you say that there's something that helps you cope with the seizures?

Positive self-talk is very important to me. When I am laying there, not able to speak, not able to move, all I have left are my thoughts. You can make them positive or negative. Sometimes when I have a seizure there are old emotions coming up. It's almost like having an "emotional flashback." The emotions from previous trauma resurface and after the seizure is over I usually end up crying really hard. I also get quite frustrated. Sometimes I'm scared and I want to hide. It varies.
My belief in God and His plan for me is my strongest motivator and biggest help. I know without a shadow of a doubt I will help others in some form or fashion.

Do you notice that anything exacerbates your seizures?

Stress is number one, especially at work. If I have a really hard half-day or full-day I am way more likely to come home and have a seizure. Chronic pain is also a trigger. I have a lower back injury from cheerleading and if I get over the pain threshold, I have a seizure.

Do you feel you've gotten support from your family and friends?

My family and I are very close - especially my mom and I. She is the one that did the research that got me into the right treatment. And for that I can never thank her enough. My friends are also like my family. But some of them have not understood. Some thought I wanted attention, or that I could control it. Some friends have been very supportive and they help me out, they know exactly what to do in emergencies. My boyfriend has also been amazing. He's helped me through so much and been someone to really lean on. He helps and encourages me to get better and I wouldn't be where I am without him.

What would you like to tell your family, friends and doctors about PNES?

I'd like to tell my mom "thank you." She's taught me how to push myself and be resilient. I would like her to know that sometimes I'm going to get upset and that that's perfectly okay, it's part of the healing process. I would tell my boyfriend that it's very scary to lose all control of your body, to sometimes feel that you don't have control of your mind. That what I need is reassurance that I'm safe because of the things I've been through, being around males can be very triggering to me. And I would tell my friends that I didn't choose this. I would really like to sit down and explain what it is and come to an understanding on both sides. Especially the ones who have moved away I think it was before we knew it was PNES and before I could really explain it. I would like to tell the medical professionals that it is important for them to listen first of all. And if this is a disease or disorder that they don't understand, to research. And to take into account that PTSD is a real thing and PNES is a real thing. No one chooses this, no one fakes it and at the end of the day we're all here to help each other.

Do you feel like you've learned something personally from having PNES?

It's taught me my own strengths, especially recently as I've gotten better. I've realized I am a whole lot stronger than I thought I was and also taught me to give up the control freak side of me that existed. I used to try to control everything I could because so much of my life was chaos and out of control so I used that to become a perfectionist and do everything I possibly could to stop bad things from happening. Because of the abuse I learned to over-analyze everything so I could stay one step ahead in hopes of not getting hurt. I have also learned some things are just not worth getting upset about. Because if I get too upset I might have a seizure, so I've learned to pick my battles.

I love this quote:
"Resilience is accepting your new reality, even if it's less good than the one you had before. You can fight it, you can do nothing but scream about what you've lost, or you can accept that and try to put together something that's good".
-Elizabeth Edwards

This quote expresses exactly what I've learned from having PNES! I am incredibly resilient and strong.
I am positive and optimistic. Instead of screaming about the life I could have without PNES I work hard to get better and live a full life as much as possible.

How was your health before you started having PNES?

The only thing I had was the lower back injury. Growing up, I was in every activity possible! This momentum continued at university. I made good grades, was president and/or head of several organizations and had a very active social life.

And then...Bam! Everything changed. PNES took away my confidence and my sense of self. I defined myself as "sick" for years. It's been within the past year that I have shed that definition to see myself as AC. I am me again. I'm not the same me I was before. In some ways I'm better; in some ways I have a lot of healing to do. But no matter what I know I am strong and I will overcome the hurdles along my path. Because of PNES, I have discovered my resiliency and ability to persevere.

What do you see in your future?

I see myself getting married, possibly with a child or thinking about children and I really do see a life without PNES. I see myself working full time as a teacher.

And I would like to tell anyone reading the book that there is hope, that no matter how bad it is, you can start to get better and your life might not look like you planned, but you can still have a good life.

MW
New Jersey
April 2015

MW is a 35 year old married woman who has three sons who are 18, 12 and 2 ½. She is originally from a country in the Caribbean. She has a college degree in English language and English literature (something akin to liberal arts) and teaching. She worked as a home health attendant for one year before having to leave her job after she fell down a long flight of stairs. She is not currently working because she developed PNES the day after she fell at work and was not able to resume working.

Diagnostic History

 I had my first seizure at the age of 33. It started from my toes, and went to my neck, I became numb, my teeth started chattering and then my eyes rolled. I was in a doctor's office. I had gone there because I had fallen down a staircase at work the day before and had hit my head, knees, back and had to be checked out. I had gone into the exam room to change my clothes and put on the gown to go and do the x-ray and suddenly this started happening. Neither my husband nor I had never had anything like that before but when the doctor came in he started yelling "she's having a seizure, she's having a seizure!" I could hear what they were saying and my husband was saying "no she doesn't have that. I don't know what going on but she doesn't have seizures". So they called the EMT's who took me to a hospital. In the ambulance I was having a lot of tremors, my teeth were chattering and my body was very cold. When so I got to the ER but they put me in the hallway for a while before moving me to the cubicle and while I was in the hallway I hear nurses and people going by and seeing my seizures.

Then they sent me to do a CT scan and they used contrast dye and suddenly I broke out in hives! We found out that day that I am allergic to that dye. After all of this, they had me rest a little, they had me in observation a little then I was discharged that night, sometime after 2am or so. I went home, took a nap and was up by say 8 o'clock. My back pain and my head still hurt and I was confused about having a seizure. They had said in the hospital that it was maybe due to hyperventilation. So that morning I started to boil some eggs for my breakfast but I forgot that the eggs were on the stove and the eggs were burned. It was the scent of that that got my husband's attention. It's like my mind wasn't really there. I decided to keep going though and that day I went to the hairdresser. But when I was under the dryer, I had the second seizure-like activity where my limbs were moving. And so my oldest son saw what was happening and said "oh my mom is having another seizure." The people in the salon have known me for years and they were afraid so they called the EMT. By the time the ambulance got there I was able to speak a little and I refused to go to the hospital because I had just been released that same morning. But when I got home, my family members insisted that I go to another hospital just to get checked out just in case. And as I was waiting in the lobby, I had my third seizure. They gave me an intravenous injection and put me to sleep and by the time I woke up I was on the stretcher and a lot of people were holding me down. My speech became very slurred and I didn't know what was going on. I was scared out of my mind thinking "why can't I speak properly, I know the words but I can't form them." And I was drooling. I was scared to death. I was very afraid because in a matter of 24 hours all these changes had happened. I spent 7 days at that hospital and while there I lost my ability to walk, I lost my ability to talk.

Initially, they thought I had postpartum depression because I had a young child. So I was evaluated by a psychiatrist. Some people thought maybe I was on drugs and was in withdrawal. I feel they thought this because of my race, since I am black. I felt, like they saw me like a crackhead, a crazy person. I felt mistreated. If I asked a question they would look at me like I was stupid. They ran blood work, x-rays, MRI's and nothing showed up. Then they did a video EEG and this woman doctor came in and said "well, the results show that you don't have epilepsy. You have something that we call pseudo-seizures." I got so upset. I said "do you think that I'm faking this? Do you think I wanna be laid up in this hospital and have someone worried about me and not be able to walk or lose my speech??" So she had to explain that when they say "faking it" (through "pseudo:") that they don't mean I'm consciously faking it, just that these are "fake seizures." But we had never heard of anything like this and it didn't make any sense to any of us. So she recommended that I see a psychologist, but my family and I were like: "I'm not seeing a psychologist, I'm not one of those people because I'm not crazy. Crazy people go to those doctors, I'm not crazy. I'm not stupid." I wasn't even listening to them anymore. So they discharged me and they did not give me a wheelchair. Once I got home I had to be picked up and put in the house and I had a disability nurse and a physical therapist. At this time, in just a few days I had had over 60 seizures.

My family and I tried to keep my spirits up. Thousands of people prayed for me, I got calls, cards, and money. All along I am thinking how did I get here? Why is this happening to me? When will I be able to walk? When can I go to the bathroom alone? When am I going to be able to bathe myself without someone having to soap up the rag and wash my back? It was so frustrating. Sometimes I thought "I cannot live like this" and other days, I said to myself "God's gonna take me through it because I'm strong." So I tried to keep positive but there were times when I was spiraling into a deep depression. I spent 7 weeks not able to walk and I had a young baby. I was forced to stop breast feeding him because they didn't know what was wrong with me. My other kids were sad, they helped take care of me by bringing me meals in bed. My oldest picked me up like a baby and carried me to the living room and put me on the couch, put me in the bathroom, took me to the toilet. We had a computer chair and I was able to sit in it and kind of wheel myself around. I also had to rent a walker from the pharmacy.

What do your seizures look like?

It was almost like somebody else took over my body, my body would arch so high that you could crawl under it, shaking, my eyes would roll over, foaming, my tongue would hang out… During one, I was shouting and speaking another language. They could last 10 minutes, 20 minutes, 30 minutes and by the time they had calmed down for 10 minutes, I might have another one. And when it ended, I had terrible muscle pain. It would be hours before I recovered. I would feel weakness, my legs would have no feelings but I would have pain in my back and my head.

What treatments have you received for PNES?

My dad's ex-wife, I call her my step-mom, attends a church where there's this pastor who believes in praying for healing. Some of my family members and friends thought that the doctors didn't know what they were talking about and even thought that maybe a ghost had pushed me down the staircase. Some people said demons like witchcraft, voodoo was happening. They thought it was demonic possession because my body would arch. It was almost as if I had no bones. My legs and upper body would open and close like when you clap, my body would fold. So this pastor prayed over me and put holy oil on me and I walked out and did not need my wheelchair anymore.

But I was still having seizures so I realized I had to look for a psychologist. It was very difficult for me to find one though. My insurance was good, they gave me at least 20 different psychologists. I called and I called and I called. And most of them said either they're no longer in network and then I went round and round calling the insurance to tell them this and being told "they're still in network, they just don't want to take you." Some other psychologists said that they were full. Others said they didn't have expertise in PNES. Some of them were just far away. Finally I found my first psychologist, who was a very caring doctor. He said "yes I'll take you." I went to see him a few times. He was first one who explained to me that when my body arched it could be re-living the very moment that I'm falling down the staircase. So all that fear that's in the back of my head, even though I might not be thinking about it, it was there subconsciously. He was a very nice doctor too. He would come down stairs to meet me at the door and he would walk upstairs with me. But once my lawyers contacted him, he explained he was not a forensic psychologist, so he gave me a 1-800 number to call three places. I got my second psychologist from there and I saw him for several months. I was doing a little better, I would have breaks from the seizures but they would come back and then in September my doctor said "I don't understand. You come once a week, we talk, but you're still having these episodes. You are not getting better. I have never had a patient come in with the same thing you have so perhaps PNES is really out of my scope. I think you need to go somewhere else where you can get the help that you need." He mentioned that he had read an article about a doctor in New York who specialized in PNES.

I remember when I finally got the name of a place where this doctor worked with PNES from him. I called that office and said "listen, I've been really struggling and this is <u>my last hope</u>. I want only the best. I want whoever's at the top" and even though she was in another state and I had to travel sometimes for 2 or more hours, I did it. She was someone who specialized in PNES as well as PTSD.

What has been your experience working with medical professionals? For example doctors and give examples if you have any.

I've had good and bad experiences with doctors. The worst is one day that I had a seizure in my physical therapy session. EMT took me to an emergency room where I was made to feel less than a dog. The ER doctor came up to me and slapped me in the face and then he turned to his nurses and told them: "See, I told you she was faking." That hard slap did kind of bring me back out of the seizure but it was very hard and hurt me, and no doctors had ever done that to me before and no doctor has ever done that again! I had spent 14 days in the hospital, two different ones and no one ever physically touched me like that. If there was such a technique they would have used it at some point at the other hospitals. When that happened I heard him say: "See, I told you she was faking it" and those words, I remember to this day. When I recovered a bit, I wrote "who was that doctor?" because I couldn't speak. I requested that they "call 911, call the police. File a report because I'm not going sit here and be treated less than a dog. Nobody would ever slap their dog." So, the police didn't come, but it was reported to the hospital director and all sorts of big people came down and got me a different doctor, got me a cubicle with curtains or whatever and they apologized and they called on the doctor. My dad came in and my dad started yelling at him. My husband wanted to knock him out. They wanted to beat him up because you know I was already in distress and to add to it and make me feel embarrassed. I heard him, it's not like someone told me he said it, I heard him. He turned around and said "she was faking it, see I told you she was faking it." I felt treated worse than an animal.

Other doctors, I felt like I was irritating them. The neurologist I had at one of the first hospitals, every time she came I was having a new pain, pins and needle, or I was losing speech. She became frustrated and said "I don't know, I don't know, I run all the tests, I don't know what else to do". So my brother got mad and said "you are supposed to help her and everyone is telling her this and that. You've got to figure what is wrong with her." When she was delivering the EEG results, she was impatient, it's like she didn't have time to stand there and explain. It was like "okay you have this disorder, that's all you need to know, that's all I have to tell you."

And my general practitioner, when I tried to return to her for follow up, she refused to see me and instead I got a "letter of dismissal." Can you believe I was dismissed as a patient without any explanation! She couldn't understand why I was not talking or walking and why I had not seen a psychologist yet.

But I have also had positive experiences with the doctors. The first other doctor, outside of the hospital, was a neurologist that we went to for a second opinion. He didn't seem to know much about PNES but he wrote me a prescription for occupational and physical therapy and he was a nice doctor.

A neurologist I saw later in another hospital when I already knew I had PNES was also kind. And my psychologists, all three of them, were good.

What treatments did you receive for PNES and how have they helped you?

It's been a long pathway to even find someone who knew about PNES. The treatments I got helped me first off because they taught me about PNES and PTSD. I had never heard of them and so I learned what they were.

Then we had to work on the PTSD. The exercises were hard, very difficult, but in the end they worked out. The in vivo, the imagery, I forget the names, were good. Breaking the memory of that fall down in fragments, that was difficult at first but got easier over time. I just kept repeating everything until I got through it all. The exercises were tricky too, first by looking at pictures of staircases, trying to look over the banister and go up and down different staircases and escalators and stuff like. And as I managed to overcome the trauma, my seizures also went away. I started to be able to go to games and public places and to stop avoiding things.

Now, I have only had two seizures in almost one year. I still feel like I need to talk to someone every now and again. I don't need extended treatment like every week, I'm doing much better in terms of the PNES and PTSD. I think that I'm doing very well now.

What benefits you the most when you're trying to cope with your seizures?

After the two seizures I had, it's become much easier for me to identify triggers immediately. After the seizure I can say "well this and this and that kind of led up to me finally having one." If I am exhausted it's more likely that I will crash.

I find that in certain situations, after treatment, I can look at things in more of a positive way, not just the negative. I don't just have the "oh my God, what am I gonna do, how am I going to fix it?" part. Now I find some way to rectify the situation instead of going into some type of panic or being worried all the time. I know that if I'm very upset it leads up to a seizure, so now I use my breathing technique. If I feel numbness in my feet, I say to myself "maybe that's going to lead up to a seizure" and I do my breathing. It won't prevent them all the time but it helps me. I also sometimes try to zone out a little bit, get into my little world and get away from everyone. Sometimes it helps to go shopping. I like to sleep too and when I'm sleeping I don't worry about anything. I also started going to the gym. I remember the first time I went I was scared to use the machine, to go upstairs. I didn't have a gym partner or anyone supervising me. But once I started exercising, I watched TV and I kind of zoned out all negativity. I was able to do it.

Would you say that you've learned something from PNES? Has PNES taught you anything?

PNES has taught me a lot. It has taught me both good and bad. But mostly good because I've met some other patients that have become my friends. The bad part for me is that it really limits my income and other activities. Whether it's going out or being in public, having dinner at the movies, being intimate. Sometimes we joke about it "oh what if you have a seizure while we're having sex" or "what if we go to the movies and you have a seizure". I've had it so many places, indoors, outdoors, I've had it in stores, at my son's football game. The embarrassment, the stigma, everyone looking at you like you're crazy, like it's your fault. Like you're faking it, because they don't understand. So what I do is I collect the PNES pamphlets at my doctor's office and I share it with other doctors and I give it to family members and I give it to anyone who is interested in it and I explain it to them about PNES.

What would you like to tell other about your PNES?

I think it's important for families to stick together, to know that they have to be patient with the individual with the diagnosis, for them to show love. It's important to try to act in a normal way, don't sugar-coat things, but don't walk around like you're stepping on eggshells. Try to understand that the person may feel very depressed and that they would like to be able to talk about something other than seizures, something other than you being sick. So I think love, patience, understanding and learning about PNES is important. Try to be there in whatever capacity you can, physically or mentally. No matter what it is, just listen, pray with this person. Just anything that you can do because I've had situations where some friends that I used to have just stopped calling and don't invite me out anymore. I remember one friend who I went to school with so I had known her a long time. One day when we were shopping and I started having the seizures. She had to go to work and EMT came and took me away. She never even called to see if I was okay after that. And I recently talked to her and I said "oh I'm doing fine" even though she didn't ask.

My sister, as close as we are, she won't let me watch her baby by myself. My husband won't give me his car to drive. Some people will invite me to lunch but then they say: "I hope you don't have a seizure then." I want them to understand that it's not up to me to have a seizure, it just happens." They don't get it and so they gossip. But I have some loyal people in the church. They help me with money, with food, everything. There are a few good ones. So it's been good and bad.

What would you want to tell doctors about what it's like to live with PNES?

I think doctors should be more aware of each and every patient. Be more sensitive and watch what you're saying. Use your words properly and explain it thoroughly and the best that you can, because when you tell a patient "oh you have x" it can be confusing. If you say: you have x but the patients doesn't know what x is, they need more information. Make sure you can say "go there, there's a support group there and there's a certain doctor here". Give them a specific reference instead of just saying "go to A psychologist". Where are the psychologists that deal with PNES? There should be a group that says "we specialize in patients with PNES." And the doctors and EMTs need to be educated. Because once they come on the scene and they realize that it's not epilepsy and it's a "pseudoseizure," they start treating you like you're a crackhead, like you're stupid, like you're faking it, like you just want attention. They are rough with you. Some are like "oh my gosh, not her again."

If you study to be a doctor, you should be aware of PNES because there are hundreds of thousands of us with this condition and we're being mistreated. For me, I've been discharged twice from psychologists for their own different reasons which I understand, I've been discharged from a physical therapist facility because of the seizures. I've been discharged from my general doctor. Even lawyers are confused.

Psychologists need to be interested and learn about PNES so they can be a part of this field. The more people who are involved, the more people will become aware of it. It's about education, education, education. Educating the public, the medical personnel and everyone across the board. We need to start having commercials on TV, now we have a ribbon and we have banners. But we need more so we can be moving on up. The goal is eventually that other persons won't look at us as crazy or faking and seeking attention. This may not be epilepsy but these seizures are as real to us, the patients, as anything. We suffer tremendously from this condition. And anyone who overcomes it, they should know that they have done an exceptional achievement in doing that.

How would you describe your quality of life since you developed PNES?

It has been hard. It's been a lot of struggle to get where I am at now and although my seizures are nearly gone, the struggle continues. Because of the seizures I lost my job and my marriage got into big trouble. In fact, I'm in the process of being evicted and because I can't go to work and pay my rent on time. We're working on patching things up with my husband but it's been tough. I felt like a tsunami happened to me and my whole life changed after that one day when I fell. My whole life changed... No workers comp coming in, no welfare money or social security, zero financial support: that was hard!

But I am getting myself back up and have plans for this year.

What do you see for your future?

I'm not gonna let PNES or PTSD beat me. I'm gonna be a winner on this one. I'm going to try to live my life as normally as possible. Once my physical problems (my back) are better, the first thing is to get a job. I'm going to start out small and go to something bigger and be able to work and pay my rent. I want to go back into teaching, maybe start as a substitute teacher. But my intention is to go back to school because I already have a diploma in teaching at the secondary level, and I need to go for a year and a half, maybe less for my Bachelor's degree in education. I want to specialize in children with disabilities. I want to be a special education teacher.

*Tell your story.
Show your example.
Tell everyone it's
possible
and others shall
feel the
courage
to climb their own
mountains.*

Paulo Coelho

Appendix

Questions for Those Living with PNES

1. Pseudonym or Initials
2. Sex
3. Age
4. Marital Status
5. Children (if any)
6. What is your highest level of education?
7. Employment status - Are you currently employed and, if not, why? Did you have to leave your job because of illness, (if so, how long ago and are you currently on disability?).
8. At what age or what year did your seizures begin?
9. Do you know why you have these seizures?
10. How was your diagnosis made and how was it explained to you by that doctor?
11. How long was it from the time your seizures began until they were correctly diagnosed?
12. What do your seizures look like? How do they present themselves? For example, do you lose consciousness, become paralyzed but remain conscious, vocalize, have spasms in your arms and/or legs? Is your speech/hearing affected and how long do your seizures last?
13. How do you feel after your seizures and what is your recovery time (minutes, hours, days)?
14. Were you diagnosed with another disorder or illness prior to being diagnosed with PNES?
15. What has been your experience in working with medical professionals, (doctors, nurses, ER physicians, EMT's,

psychiatrists, neurologists, psychologists, social workers, etc.). Give examples if you have some.
16. How would you rate or describe your quality of life?
17. What benefits you the most when coping with your seizures?
18. What exacerbates your seizures?
19. Do you feel that you have the understanding and support of your friends and family in dealing with your illness?
20. What would you like to tell others in your life, your family, your friends and your medical professionals, about what it's like to live with PNES and what they can do to help you to heal from this illness?
21. What have you learned, personally, from having PNES?
22. Other comments…

For further information and resources please contact:

Lorna Myers, Ph.D.
Northeast Regional Epilepsy Group
Director, Psychogenic Non-epileptic Seizure Program
Executive Director, Epilepsy Free Foundation
Associate Director of Epilepsy Life Links
820 Second Avenue, Suite 6C
New York, New York 10017
212-661-7460

www.epilepsygroup.com
http://nonepilepticseizures.com/
http://blog.nonepilepticseizures.com/

Available on amazon.com:
Psychogenic non-epileptic seizures: A Guide
Lorna Myers, Ph.D.

Printed in Great Britain
by Amazon